# Pond on the Prairie

Ronald James Newton

**Gotham Books**

30 N Gould St.
Ste. 20820, Sheridan, WY 82801
https://gothambooksinc.com/

Phone: 1 (307) 464-7800

© 2025 *Ronald James Newton*. All rights reserved.

No part of this book may be reproduced, stored in a retrieval system, or transmitted by any means without the written permission of the author.

Published by Gotham Books (March 5, 2025)

ISBN: 979-8-3482-6910-4 (P)
ISBN: 979-8-3482-6911-1 (E)

Because of the dynamic nature of the Internet, any web addresses or links contained in this book may have changed since publication and may no longer be valid.

The views expressed in this work are solely those of the author and do not necessarily reflect the views of the publisher, and the publisher hereby disclaims any responsibility for them.

South Platte River, Weld County, Colorado, *Sheila Koenig*, 2015

*Cover Photograph:*

*Cover photo AI-generated by the author using the IStock Photo Gallery*

*Dedicated to Lydia Heist Dreier, James Elmer Newton, Laura Celia Dreier Newton, Raymond Lee Newton, and Marcus Emerit Newton; their lives are the inspirational basis for the content of this story.*

Raymond Lee Newton
*1937 Newton Family Album*

Marcus Emerit Newton
*2003 Newton Family Album*

Laura Celia Dreier Newton and James Elmer Newton 1941

*Newton Family Album*

Lydia Heist Dreier

*Mother of Laura Dreier Newton*
*1938 Newton Family Album*

*Proverbs 1:8 - Listen, my son, to your father's instruction and do not forsake your mother's teaching.*

*Thanks to Marcus Emerit Newton for editing the manuscript.*

*Thanks to Patricia Thornton Lewis for designing the cover.*

*Thanks to Helen Newton Teter who provided genealogical background and perspective.*

# CONTENTS

Chapter 1 .................................................................................................. 1
Chapter 2 .................................................................................................. 3
Chapter 3 .................................................................................................. 5
Chapter 4 .................................................................................................. 8
Chapter 5 ................................................................................................ 10
Chapter 6 ................................................................................................ 12
Chapter 7 ................................................................................................ 15
Chapter 8 ................................................................................................ 17
Chapter 9 ................................................................................................ 19
Chapter 10 .............................................................................................. 22
Chapter 11 .............................................................................................. 26
Chapter 12 .............................................................................................. 29
Chapter 13 .............................................................................................. 33
Chapter 14 .............................................................................................. 35
Chapter 15 .............................................................................................. 39
Chapter 16 .............................................................................................. 41
Chapter 17 .............................................................................................. 46
Chapter 18 .............................................................................................. 47
Chapter 19 .............................................................................................. 51
Chapter 20 .............................................................................................. 54
Chapter 21 .............................................................................................. 57
Chapter 22 .............................................................................................. 61
Chapter 23 .............................................................................................. 64
Chapter 24 .............................................................................................. 68
Chapter 25 .............................................................................................. 72
Chapter 26 .............................................................................................. 74
Chapter 27 .............................................................................................. 76
Chapter 28 .............................................................................................. 80
Chapter 29 .............................................................................................. 83
Chapter 30 .............................................................................................. 87
Chapter 31 .............................................................................................. 90
Chapter 32 .............................................................................................. 94
Chapter 33 .............................................................................................. 96
Chapter 34 .............................................................................................. 99
Chapter 35 ............................................................................................ 101
Chapter 36 ............................................................................................ 103
Chapter 37 ............................................................................................ 105
Chapter 38 ............................................................................................ 108

Chapter 39 ............................................................................... 111
Chapter 40 ............................................................................... 114
Chapter 41 ............................................................................... 116
Chapter 42 ............................................................................... 119
Chapter 43 ............................................................................... 122
Chapter 44 ............................................................................... 125
Chapter 45 ............................................................................... 128
Chapter 46 ............................................................................... 131
Chapter 47 ............................................................................... 133
Chapter 48 ............................................................................... 136
Chapter 49 ............................................................................... 139
Chapter 50 ............................................................................... 143
Chapter 51 ............................................................................... 145
Chapter 52 ............................................................................... 148
Chapter 53 ............................................................................... 149
Chapter 54 ............................................................................... 153
Chapter 55 ............................................................................... 155
Chapter 56 ............................................................................... 158
Chapter 57 ............................................................................... 162
Chapter 58 ............................................................................... 165

# 1

The United States Prairie, an area of rolling and flat grasslands, spans eastward from the Rocky Mountains into America's midsection and extends north to Canada and south to Mexico. That stretch emanating from the Front Range and expanding over most of eastern Colorado is part of the shortgrass prairie ecosystem. Due to increasing aridity and drought, the shortgrass prairie evolved over the last twenty million years from an open forest with occasional grassy areas to an open grassland with few trees. Dominated by blue grama and buffalo grass interspersed with yucca and prickly pear, the shortgrass prairie became the feeding ground of huge herds of free-ranging bison, antelope, deer, and elk, supporting predatory gray wolves and grizzly bears. The shortgrass prairie was also home to many underground colonies of prairie dogs and many birds, including sparrows, shrikes, hawks, owls, plovers, and longspurs.

In the early 1800s and as the warmer days of spring arrived, the Colorado prairie became the hunting ground of the Arapaho who resided in the protective area of Boulder Valley during the winter months. Tribal leader, Chief Niwot, led his party onto the shortgrass prairie plains, hunting bison gathering for the birthing season. In midsummer, they traveled into the higher elevated parks region to hunt mountain herds of deer and elk. In late summer and early autumn, they returned to the prairie plains for collective hunts of herds gathering for the rutting season, including antelope. As they veered eastward, they often set up camp on the southern bank of the South Platte River. When their hunting pursuits took them further south, they camped on a small pond, thirty or so miles from the River. The pond, with a surface area of a couple of acres, was sustained year-round by spring water bubbling up from a large underground aquifer. The Arapaho aptly named this tiny body of water, ***konoote' coo'oowse,'*** i.e., "Bubbling Pond."

The water had a bright blue hue, which radiated magnificently as the sun disappeared from the horizon. To the Arapaho, it was ***huno'ceneeteeyoo' nec*** (blue-sky water), that had been purified by their ancestral spirits, in preparation for them to drink. The sound from a constant vertical movement of aqueous globules to the surface was a communication sign from their buried forefathers. This site was sacred – and in the evening by the light of the campfire, they stomped to the beat of the drum celebrating the success of their hunting quests, and they prayed in thanksgiving:

*Oh Great Spirit*
*We give thanks for the grass of the prairie*
*It supports the bison and the antelope*
*Whose skins cover our bodies*
*Whose flesh feeds us*
*Their abundance is a gift from you*
*You provide favor to our people*
*We are grateful*

# 2

In 1852 Max Wilhelm hopped on a stagecoach at Holyoke, Colorado, early one April morning. He was on his way to Sterling to visit a German-speaking aunt who had immigrated to the United States from Canada's Ontario Province. His Aunt Ernestine had married a banker and inherited a rightful sum when he died. The aim of eighteen-year-old Wilhelm, the firstborn of immigrant German parents, was to borrow enough money from his aunt to pay the filing fee, buy a homestead, and begin a farming career. He had promised his fiancé that he would marry her as soon as he had homesteaded and had constructed a house on the premises. The stagecoach headed east out of Holyoke onto the prairie grassland – plush green and vibrant from spring rains. The grass carpet of buffalo grama sparkled dazzlingly with dew, and the early morning sun reflected from the flowering morning glory and yucca, spread in brilliant patches of red-purple and white all over the expansive green landscape.

The coach stopped at Haxtun and then at Fleming. About twenty miles west of Fleming, Wilhelm spotted an antelope taking a drink of water from a pond about a half-mile away. As the stage approached, the antelope bolted and ran away, disappearing across the prairie. The driver stopped the coach, pausing to allow his horses to recharge their dehydrated bodies. Wilhelm exited to stretch his legs and to view the pond and the surrounding prairie.

"That water is sure a purty blue," exclaimed Wilhelm as he stared across the pond.

"It sure is," said the driver. "They say it is so pure – it is safe to drink it. I always bring my water, so I've never tried it."

"You know the grass around here looks healthy – I think a feller could farm out here and make a go of it. Doncha reckon?"

"I think he could," agreed the driver.

Wilhelm received his loan and walked to the Logan County make-shift, wood-sided courthouse and homesteaded 640 acres including Bubbling Pond, close to its eastern border. Six months later, he and his wife were living in a limestone brick house on the west side of the pond. He still allowed the stagecoach-run to traverse his property, and the run stop became known as Wilhelm Station.

# 3

In the late 1700s, ethnic Germans, ravaged by the wars of the German states and suffering from religious strife and economic hardship, immigrated to Russia, encouraged by Catherine the Great. A hundred years later, Russia passed legislation that revoked many of the privileges promised to them by Catherine. While Russia was reducing privileges granted to these German settlers, overtures were made from Canada and America offering inducements and encouraging them to immigrate. Many German-speaking Protestant and Catholic German-Russians immigrated to Canada's Ontario province and America's heartland. The immigrants were often of the same village and traveled together across the Atlantic and settled together in their new homeland. Because of the opportunity for irrigation farming, a large number of German-Catholic families decided to homestead on land surrounding Wilhelm Station. Another sizeable group of German Lutherans also settled in the area, choosing to be merchants and starting businesses.

The land between Fleming and Sterling quickly became known as an optimum farming area, and soon homesteaders were settling in and starting farm operations. The territory was particularly attractive to settlers from Canada – second-generation folks whose parents had migrated from Germany and were now adults and ready to embrace a farming livelihood. German migration to the area was enhanced also by a financier/entrepreneur, Albert Klein, who homesteaded two sections, one next to Max Wilhelm and Bubbling Pond. Knowing the Burlington and Missouri Railroad was anticipating building a line that was to run by Wilhelm Station, Klein platted a portion of his land for a township and began to sell lots to potential homeowners. German Canadians and

German Russians flocked to Wilhelm Station to build homes and establish businesses. The wealthy Klein bought up land in Colorado and Nebraska, selling it for a handsome profit to the railroad, which expanded the line all the way from Kearney, Nebraska to Denver. Klein invested heavily in B&MR, becoming its primary stockholder. Being asthmatic, he moved to Colorado seeking relief, and he settled in Wilhelm Station to be with his German peers. His towering mansion overlooked Bubbling Pond. Klein, growing up in Canada as the only son of a wealthy medical doctor, was educated at Harvard, having earned an undergraduate degree in philosophy and a law degree. Albert Klein practiced law, and with his wealth and business acumen, soon became the dominant voice in the community.

Starting first with just a grocery store serving the local immigrant population in 1872, the town began to grow. Tom Baker, a native of Kansas, built a ground-floor grocery store with above-living quarters one block from Bubbling Pond. The post office was set up in the back of Bass's Drugs – Bob Bass was appointed postmaster. Bill Davenport started Klein Hardware. Montgomery Ward established a branch store on Main Street. Two restaurants and a bar opened. By 1890, the population was nearly four hundred and was spread over an area of one square mile. People from all around began to refer to the town as "Klein ville" – they no longer called it Wilhelm Station – that name was soon to be forgotten – after many years, the town on the shore of Bubbling Pond was known simply as "Klein."

Bubbling Pond was the only water source for the thriving community. Albert Klein, realizing this, offered to buy the pond and surrounding acreage from Wilhelm. Wanting to pay off his land loan debt, Wilhelm accepted Klein's offer. As Klein grew in numbers, Bubbling Pond could not supply the domestic needs of its residents. Klein decided to build a ditch from the South Platte River and transport water to Bubbling Pond. He formed a company and with hired help surveyed and plowed a shallow area where the ditch was to go. He "put the word out" that anyone who came to dig would receive ten dollars' worth of stock in the company for each day's work – two dozen men with horse teams showed up. After several days, thirty-one miles of ditch had been completed, and water from the South Platte was diverted to Bubbling Pond. Klein converted Bubbling Pond into a reservoir by enlarging it and building a dike on one side – bringing a large scope of farmers into irrigation agriculture. As its volume increased, Bubbling Pond lost its blue hue, and the rising aqueous globules, although presumed to be produced, could not be seen from the shore. Nevertheless, Bubbling Pond became the legendary landmark of the community and was the venue for a variety of recreational activities, including fishing, swimming, ice skating, and picnicking.

In 1913 Albert Klein was elected to the state legislature on the Republican ticket. During the time he was a member of the legislature, he was chairman of the important committee on irrigation and secured the passage of a bill that was to become the foundation of all irrigation laws of Colorado.

# 4

The flow of water from the South Platte into the diked-up Bubbling Pond enlarged the surface area from a couple of acres to twenty. Klein supplied water to surrounding farms via two ditches originating from an outlet carved out of the dike on the south side of the pond. By Colorado legislative law, each farm homestead was assured an annual allotted portion of water for irrigation purposes. Payment was made to Klein, because the law stated that whoever diverted the water, owned the water rights. Klein also sold water to the township, which charged its citizens for its use. Supplying a domestic water supply required the town to construct a water tower on the north side – a silo-like cylinder – approximately twenty-five feet in diameter and ninety feet tall – crowned with a shallow, pointed, round top – painted a gun-metal gray. Printed in large, white, block letters right below the conical top, was the word "KLEIN."

Always an entrepreneur, Klein stocked Bubbling Pond with fish – blue gill, crappie, perch, and sunfish. He hired workers to build six-foot-long long tub-boats and a boat dock. He rented the boats to green-horn fishers, usually city folks – from Sterling and from across the Nebraska border, nearby Sidney. Under his encouragement, the town constable pursued poachers. Klein provided a sandy beach and picnic tables on the east shore. In the summer, from a concession stand, workers sold soda, hot-dogs, hamburgers and candy to anglers and picnickers, sunbathers, and swimmers. Bubbling Pond bustled with recreational activity throughout the summer. Klein sold lots to incoming folks on the west and north shores of Bubbling Pond, and they built houses either of wood or limestone or a combination of both. Some built coops and barns alongside their dwellings, raising chickens and milk cows to supplement their food supply.

# 5

The US Stock market crashed in October 1929, and the downfall began the Great Depression that lasted into the next decade of the 1930s. By 1936, Walter and Lara Knoblauch, who had married in 1920, had brought ten children into the world – two had died in infancy – eight had survived those harsh economic times. Lara had had one multiple birth – a set of fraternal male twins.

Lara had been raised on a 320-acre dryland farm about five miles south of Fleming, on a homestead established by her father, Lukas Dieffenbach. Lukas, a Canadian, growing up in a farming community outside of Toronto, migrated to America with his wife, Dora, along with other homesteaders of German descent. Walter and Lara met at a picnic on the grounds of St. Peter's Catholic Church, in the tiny settlement of St. Petersburg southwest of Fleming. Walter, also a Canadian, had just returned from Europe, serving as an infantry soldier alongside his British counterparts on the Western Front of World War I. Unscathed and with the War over, Walter migrated to America to visit his cousin whose Canadian father had homesteaded near St. Petersburg. Walter and Lara were married in St. Peter's in November of 1920.

Working as a hired hand on dryland farms surrounding Fleming over the last sixteen years, the Knoblauch's lived in houses on those farms as well as in rental units in Fleming. Walter, still hoping to set up a farming operation of his own, reasoned that the opportunities for success were greater with irrigation farming, and he moved his family to Klein in the fall of 1936. Having no vehicle of his own, he commandeered his cousin Leon to move Lara and his eight children and him and their belongings in the confines of Leon's flatbed '35 Ford truck.

Addressing his Cousin Leon, Walter said, "I can find more work around Klein – much more than near Fleming. I'm told there is always somethin' goin' on – they always need workers. They say the economy is improvin,' and the Depression is just about over. I hope they're right."

"Where ya goin' to live?" asked Leon.

"Ya know about that big rich guy, Albert Klein, who they say founded Klein, the town?" Walter asked.

"Yal – everybody's heard of him. I do not think he founded Klein, but he certainly has made it grow."

"Well, he advertised in Sterling's Journal Advocate that he had a house for rent – it's located on Bubbling Pond – I called him up and told him I'd take it – I think the kids and Lara will like it."

# 6

As the Great Depression held the Knoblochs in its clutches, many Klein residents were affected as well. Many could not pay their mortgages, and First National Bank foreclosed on them – they simply walked away from their homes and left town. Albert Klein "picked up" their loans and assumed ownership of several abandoned houses. One of these was a small bungalow built on the west shore of Bubbling Pond – it was the one he rented to the Knobloch's. It was a four-room cottage with a screened porch facing the water. Lara and Walter shared one bedroom with Steffi (age 3 years). Lukas (age – 15 years) and Kristoff (age 13 years) slept on the porch. The twins, Kurt and Konrad (age – 8 years), Stefan (age – 7 years), and Raimund (age – 10 years), slept in one room, while Hanna (age – 12 years) had a bed in the "living room" that had a coal-burning stove, supplying much-needed heat in the winter months. The fourth room, the kitchen, was small, with just enough space for a table and chairs, a cook stove, and a sink. The sink was equipped with running water and a drainpipe eliminating wastewater to the outside. An "outhouse" was located thirty yards from the pond shore and twenty yards from the house. With temperatures freezing and below, Lukas and Kristoff slept indoors on the living room couch that was disassembled into a bed.

"Although this living space is purty small, the rent cost of $25 a month is something we can handle as long as I can find work," said Walter to his family as the ten of them sat around the supper table one evening. "Ole man Klein is pretty strict – he charges a $10 fee if you are late with the rent check – he wants his money on the first of the month."

"I like livin' near the water," said Hanna.

"So do I," exclaimed Kristoff."

"Don't you ever go near the water without getting' your Dad's or my permission first," said Lara. "Especially you young-uns. If we can't watch over you, Lukas, you'll be responsible to watch over them – you're the oldest, and you know how to swim."

"You birds (how Lara collectively referred to her brood) – eat that sausage and sauerkraut – if you don't, I'll feed it to you again tomorrow."

Lara did not pass out compliments to others, particularly her children – but she felt complimented when her brood voraciously devoured what she prepared for meals. She could cook anything and make it acceptable to her family's taste buds. She was proud of the fact that she had been able to provide enough food for her family through the Depression. Growing up on a dryland farm outside of Fleming, she had learned to can – she brought over 150 jars of canned produce with her – they were now stored in the cellar a few yards from their new house.

"Kristoff – eat up – I know you like sauerkraut – you're a growin' boy, and you need your vegetables."

"I'm full, Mom," Kristoff retorted.

"I'll have another sausage link," said Kurt.

"Ya know what Grandpa calls these sausages?" Hanna asked the group.

"I know," interjected Kristoph. "He sez '*bratwurst*.'"

"That's what they call it in the old country," said Lara.

"Where in Germany is Grandpa from?" asked Lukas.

"His father was born on a farm outside of Munich."

"I'd like to visit that place someday," said Lukas.

Reluctantly, Walter interjected, "Perhaps you will – there's talk that Roosevelt goin' to get us in a war – an' he's goin' to start draftin' young men – he could come after you."

"I hope not," said Lukas. "I want to go to college – I want to go to CU and study journalism. I don't want to fight no war."

"I don't wantcha fightin' either," said Lara. "I'm praying that we'll stay out of the fight."

"Me too," said Walter. "I thought that when we whipped the Germans in World War I, we taught them a lesson, but I'm afraid that ain't so – here they are – startin' the fight again. Back then in Canada, I had to register when I was seventeen – then they drafted me when I was eighteen. All our fighting was in France."

"By the way, Dad," said Raimund, looking at Walter, "Gunther told me at school today that our parish is goin' to get a church building. He said his Dad was on a committee, and they're lookin' to see if they can move one here."

"I heard the same thing at the KC (Knights of Columbus) meeting the other night," said Walter. I believe it's goin' to happen."

"We sure need one – I'm gettin' tired of meetin' in that old warehouse," said Raimund.

"Who owns that building anyhow?" asked Lukas.

"Albert Klein does," said Walter. "He owns about all that property this side of the tracks. He took it over when many of those businesses went belly-up."

# 7

Walter Knobloch and three other members of the St. Boniface Catholic parish took the train to Sterling. They were asked by parish pastor, Father Gerhardt Danziger, to prepare the church building the parish had bought from the Church of Christ, for transport by train to Klein. The Church of Christ had constructed a new brick building in Sterling and were no longer in need of the 35 foot wide by 75 foot long wood structure with a 65 foot tower that had served them well for nearly fifty years. It was a block from the Burlington and Missouri Railroad tracks that connected west with Klein. Albert Klein, a stock owner, and a board member of the B&M RR offered manpower and wheeled flatbed vehicles for transport of the building to a railway flat car.

"We have the expertise to help out," said Klein to Fr. Gerhardt. "We have a standard charge for things like this – our administrative officer says it will cost your parish five hundred dollars."

"We have the money," said Fr. Gerhardt. "We have been taking a second collection at every Sunday mass for the last five years. We've been prayin' for this – the Lord has answered our prayers – this is a monumental event for our parish."

"Well, you Catholics could be helped more if you spent more time readin' the Bible – that's what we Lutherans do," Klein railed. When we're in need, we go to the Scriptures. I understand you folks don't read the Bible much."

"The Mass we say every Sunday includes passages from the Old and New Testaments – but admittedly, our parishioners need to read the Bible more frequently," responded Fr. Gerhardt. "Our church hierarchy is working on this."

The acquired church building, mounted on a flat car, was accompanied by the four church members and several rail workers in a separate passenger car on a train traveling west to Klein. Men from the parish had already poured the foundation on a lot two blocks from Bubbling Pond and next to the east side of the railroad tracks. The lot formerly was the location of a feed supply building that had been torn down – it was bought from none other than Albert Klein.

The Church of Christ had well-maintained the building – the tongue and groove wood siding had received a fresh coat of paint. The interior was wainscoted with brick-patterned linoleum, and the upper walls and ceiling were covered with a tan fiberboard. The windows were opaque-splinter glass of a cream color. Some of the tile block-linoleum pieces from the floor were missing, and some were peeling around the edges. The upper surfaces of the pinewood pews, worn from use, displayed patches of exposed bare wood.

"We'll need to replace the whole floor with new tile," Fr. Gerhardt said. "Hopefully, some day we can replace the windows with stained glass – but that will have to wait."

"I can build the altar for you," said Walter. "Give me your design and dimensions – "I can get Otto Muller to help me – he's one of the best cabinet makers in town. I'm sure he can help us recruit parishioners to help with refinishing the pews.

# 8

As the influx of the various German contingents moved to the Klein region, they brought with them stone masons with assured knowledge about the building potential of limestone and a strong inclination to use it. For Klein Lutherans, their church built of local limestone, was to be a visible reflection of their reverence to God and the Scriptures. For Albert Klein, the Zion Lutheran Church was to be the seminal architectural structure of the town; he bankrolled the endeavor and supplied two primary lots for its construction on Main Street. He hired an architect who had designed a Lutheran cathedral in St. Louis with two steeples. Said Klein, "I want one of the steeples to be so high that it can be seen from miles around – I want it to be higher than the water tower – I want it to be the primary feature of the skyline."

The brick, obtained from limestone bluffs outside of town, was sculptured with axe flattened cut marks both inside and out. For lintels, sills, and quoins, special chisels were used, supplying an element of style and artistic beauty to the structure. The inside walls were plastered with liquefied limestone powder. The church itself was a massive Gothic style structure that rested on a raised, limestone basement. The front was abutted by two front towers of differing heights. The building was cruciform in plan and in keeping with a centuries-old tradition of church architecture, its altar end faced east. The stone was laid to give diverse types of decorative detailing, such as: projecting horizontal courses, quoin corners, sides of window openings, and headings over the Gothic arches. Stained glass windows were prominent in the sanctuary including the Luther Rose – a widely known symbol of Lutheranism; Christ Kneeling in Agony in the Garden with the passage from Luke 22:42 – "Not my will, but yours be done;"

and a figure of Martin Luther, the Father of the Reformation, nailing the 99 Theses on the door of the Castle Church in Germany. Fine, natural oak and ash hardwoods were used extensively to richly embellish the spacious interior. One of the focal points was a spectacular, raised wooden pulpit with a richly carved wooden canopy. The pastor ascended to the pulpit by an amazing, twisting, wooden staircase – it was a masterpiece of the German woodworkers' craft.

# 9

Klein sent a letter to Walter Knobloch inviting him to his office – he had an important conversation that he needed to have with him. "Thanks for comin' in, Knobloch," said Klein, as he pointed to a leather chair in front of his large maple desk that he wanted him to sit in. "I want to talk about the "pond house."

"Okay, Sir," answered Walter.

"I have to ask you to vacate it – you see, I've hired a new ditch rider for Bubbling Pond, and I've promised him that house to live in as part of his salary."

"I see," said Walter – grimacing as he brought his hands to his face.

"When do you want us out?"

"By September first – that's when the rider starts."

"Have ya' got any other place for us to live?"

"The only other thing I have available is the old warehouse down by the tracks where the Catholic church used to meet. It could accommodate your large family – it has running water, a kitchen, a cooking stove, a heater, and an outhouse – would that be suitable for you?"

"What's the charge for the rent?"

"Thirty-five dollars a month."

"My God, Klein, that's ten bucks more than I'm payin' now."

"Business is business, Walter – the Depression has been hard on us all."

"Ya got me between a rock and a hard place," exclaimed Walter. "I guess I'll have to take it – where do I get the keys?"

"See my secretary on the way out – she'll give them to you."

It was the end of August when Walter moved Lara and his eight children into the warehouse. He had partitioned off three bedrooms, a living room, and the kitchen with ceiling-hanging curtains he had bought from the Second-Hand Store.

I'm sure goin' to miss the "pond house," Raimund uttered as he set down a box of books.

"We all will – we'll just have to make this do until we work somethin' out," said Lara.

"I bet the train's goin' to sound really loud here," Hanna blurted out. "How many times does it go by at night?"

"I think twice," Raimund answered.

"Lukas, you'll have to go back and get the stuff out of the cellar," Lara asserted.

Lara asked herself, "How many times have I moved with this bunch in the last twenty years?" She couldn't count them – it was too many! She was pregnant again – she felt more than one urchin churning in her bloated belly – she calculated the event to be next month. She thought about the pain she would endure – she remembered the last twin's birth; the second one's birth was a little easier. She tolerated pain well – both emotionally and physically – no one ever saw her cry. "Another set of twins again!" she contemplated. "God is blessing us – but he sure is placing a burden on us all." She reminded herself to have Walter repaint the two baskets and their holders he had made for twins Kurt and Konrad. Lara had been told many times that her strong German heritage gave her an advantage – she believed that – after all she already bore ten children – all at home - now she was thirty-eight years old, but still physically, mentally, and spiritually strong.

At ten in the evening on September 28$^{th}$, Walter sent Raimund over to the Main St. home/office of Dr. Shäfer to ask him to come quickly – Lara's water had broken. He commandeered Hanna to the house of spinster midwife, Helga Holzer, to alert her of the pending birth – her help was needed. At 11:42 pm the first twin appeared – a girl; at 12:31 am a second girl was born – *i*dentical to the first. The next day, Lara and Walter named them Kerstin and Katrin.

# 10

In July 1942, Lara Knobloch received a morning phone call from Mayor Tom Baker, owner of the Red & White Grocery Store.

"Mrs. Knobloch, are any of your boys available to mow my lawn around the store? I haven't time to do it. It'll take a couple of hours – I'll pay him 30 cents an hour."

"I think so, Mr. Baker – I think Raimund is all caught up with his house chores here – I think he could do it."

"Okay, have him see me here in the store, and I'll show him how to start up the mower."

When finished mowing, Raimund stopped by Bass's Drug Store on his way home – he wanted to buy a spiral notebook – he was going to start keeping a diary. Brother Lukas, who at the time was enrolled in Colorado University's journalism program, shared some advice: "One of my creative writing professors said, 'If you want to be a writer – keeping a diary is good training for you'." Raimond emulated Lukas – he regretted Lukas had to drop out of CU – he was now in the Marines fighting the Japanese somewhere in the South Pacific. Raimund bought two notebooks – he was certain he would be filling them up in a fleeting time.

Raimund, now 13 years old, was looking forward to the fall – he would be enrolling in high school for the first time. He loved schoolwork – he realized he was good at academics when they moved him up to a grade three years ago. But he was not the only one who was accelerated – Albert Klein's daughter, Heidi, went with him. Raimund had known Heidi since the first grade, but they were only casual friends – they saw each other infrequently. Raimond was excited about joining the new orchestra. The school had hired music teacher, Fritz Werner, with the assignment of getting the orchestra started. Lukas had left his clarinet behind – he had played in the marching band – Lara assured Raimond that Lukas would readily approve if he made use of it.

On the first day of school in orchestra class, he sat next to Heidi – she was aspiring to be a violinist. Sixteen students were enrolled. Mr. Werner announced that the class would be taking a field trip in November to Sterling. The Denver Symphony Orchestra was touring Colorado and they would be performing in the Civic Center in a matinee afternoon production – only for students from around the area.

On November 19th after an early lunch in the cafeteria, Mr. Werner boarded his 16 students onto a yellow Thomas school bus and headed to Sterling. Raimond sat with Heidi in a double seat in the small, twenty-four-passenger bus.

"My father ran into Mr. Werner in the hardware store two weeks ago," said Heidi. "He told my father the Denver Orchestra was going to feature Mozart. My father sez that is some of the most difficult music in the world to play," exclaimed Heidi. "He listens to classical music all the time – sez he learned to appreciate it when he was at Harvard. He plays records of famous composers on his Victrola in his office. Father was the one who got this orchestra program going – he's on the school board."

"My dad likes country music," said Raimund. "He listens to the Grand Ole Opry every Saturday night. He sez country music from America was big in Canada when he was growing up. Marty Robbins was one of his favorite singers."

"How 'bout you? Do you like classical?"

"I don't know – I don't know much about it – that's why I'm in the orchestra. My father sez I'll get a good understanding of classical by playing the violin – he insisted I choose the violin as the instrument to play."

"I'm usin' my brother's clarinet," said Raimund. "It was given to him by Mr. Bass when he worked for him at the drugstore – Mr. Bass had when he was young. It's old, but Lukas took good care of it – I'm really lookin' forward to learning how to play it. Mom sez I can take private lessons if I need to – sez she'll figure out how to pay for 'em. I'm goin' to sing in the choir at church – Mom sez I have a good voice – she plays the organ, and my sister Hanna sings."

"Where do you worship?" asked Heidi.

"St. Boniface – I'm Catholic."

"You sing a lot of Latin hymns there, don't you? My father hates that music – he sez the best thing about the Lutherans splitting away from the Catholics was they then developed their own music – he thinks German Lutheran hymns are superior to those of the Catholics."

"Maybe so – Mom tells me you Protestants, and I presume you Lutherans, sing more than we do – in our church the choir does most of the singing – we parishioners don't sing much – we just listen."

At Sterling, hundreds of students assembled in the auditorium in the afternoon to hear the DSO conductor discuss characteristics of classical music and to see individual members and groups of musicians to help prove his point. He pointed out certain musical phrases unique to Mozart. That night Mr. Werner and his students attended the concert – the house was full. It featured Wolfgang Amadeus Mozart's Clarinet Concerto in A Major. Raimund was mesmerized and so was Heidi. What they heard led them to a part of the world they had never experienced before. Raimond remembered what Mr. Werner had told them about classical music: "It allows you to do your own interpretations, and it always takes you to different places."

The next morning at breakfast Raimund told Lara of the great excitement and exhilaration he had felt the night before; Lara smiled – she was happy – she knew exactly what he was talking about. She recalled how invigorated she was when her father sat her down next to him and taught her to play the organ.

# 11

September 1942

09/1. School starts in a week. I can hardly wait.

09/2. Finished weeding and hoeing Mr. Baker's garden; had been working on it for 3 days – he paid me 30 cents/hr.– I earned a total of $7.20. Mr. Baker complimented me on the fine job I had done – tipped me $.80 – I put $8.00 in my pocket. We talked about reading books – he likes "westerns" – his favorite author is Louis L'Amour. I told him I wanted to be a writer. He said, "Keep focused on it – write whenever you can - someday it will happen."

09/3. Went to Schuster's Department Store to shop for school clothes. Bought two pairs of jeans, 5 pairs of underwear, 5 T-shirts and 3 sports shirts. Mom supplemented my $8.00 budget with $3.00.

09/4. This freshman year I'll be taking geometry. Finished Algebra 1 last year. I like math, but English is my favorite subject.

09/5. Saw the school principal in the drugstore. He told me he hired a new English teacher this year. He said he was a recent graduate of Colorado State College of Education.

09/6. Went to church – Mom played the new organ – a gift from the Bishop in celebration of getting the new building. Hanna and I sang in the choir.

9/7. First day of school – wore new shirt Mom made for me – green plaid – sat next to Heidi Klein in orchestra class. Showed my clarinet to Mr. Werner – he marveled at its great condition. The new English teacher, Thomas Trever, is from Denver – said he will be giving us a writing assignment soon – wanted us to start thinking about a topic.

09/8. Saturday – no school. This morning I walked to St. Boniface for confession – confessed sin committed ("talking back to Mom") – an offense against the fourth commandment (Honor thy father and mother). This afternoon, I swept and scrubbed the living room floor for Mom and dusted the furniture.

09/9. Went to church and sang in the choir – washed dishes after a big dinner. Mom prepared ham and sweet potatoes. Have a feeling we'll be having ham and pinto beans tomorrow night.

09/10. On my way home from school today, paused to watch a pelican consume a school of minnows on Bubbling Pond. Unusual to see pelicans here – they usually are seen on the Sterling Reservoir – was the poor soul lost?

09/11. Swept drugstore floors after school. Took 2 hours. Mr. Bass pays me 50 cents an hour. Wants me to stock shelves tomorrow – just got in a load of school supplies.

09/12. Mom reminded me to practice my clarinet. She remarked she was glad that it was still warm weather so I could do it outside (she didn't want to listen to me).

# 12

Walter finished stacking hay on Oliver Berger's farm early in the afternoon, and he asked Berger to drop him off at Bakers R&W so he could pick up a can of Prince Albert and a book of cigarette papers. He always stopped off at R&W because he knew Tom Baker would cash his paycheck.

"Walter, I heard you're wantin' to get out of that warehouse and are lookin' for a house. Is that right?" asked Baker.

"I sure am!" exclaimed Walter, as he accepted the several bills and change in his left palm. "The missus is about go insane in that place with no privacy. In the wintertime ya' can't heat it – it's always cold, and there's rats and mice all around. My little Steffi cries at night when she hears 'em – scared she's' goin' to get bitten. And ole man Klein is chargin' me an 'arm and a leg' for that God-forsaken hell-hole."

"Well, do you know about that limestone, two-story house over on Fifth St. with the unpainted, shingle roof? You know the one that ole Kruger couple lived in?"

"Yal – I've seen it."

"As you know, they both died, and it's now in the hands of the tax office – I guess they didn't have any kids or relatives they could pass it on to. Thinkin' I might buy it, I called Sterling to see how much the lien was on it. They said it was sixteen hundred – hadn't paid taxes for many years. I went over to look at it, and when I saw how big it was, I thought of you Knobloch's with your big family. It's just perfect for you folks. If you want it, I'll let you have the first choice, if you like. You need it more than I do."

"How many rooms does it have?" asked Walter.

"Seven – three upstairs and four downstairs. Will need some paintin' and fixin' up a bit."

"M-My gosh, T-Tom," Walter stammered. "That's mighty nice of you. You sure you don't want it?"

"I want you to have it – you've got a nice family, and you all deserve it."

The next day, Walter made an appointment at First National to secure a loan – he had no savings. The young loan officer said, "Normally, we take all loan requests to the board, but since you want me to speed up it, I guess I could ask for Mr. Klein's approval. He's not here right now, but he's usually over in his law office – I can call over there and see if he can see us."

Walter and the loan officer, Jack Leonard, sat down in front of Klein's sprawling, walnut desk. A framed Harvard law degree diploma hung on the wall to the right where Klein was sitting. There was a picture of Klein with the Colorado governor, Ed Johnson, on his left. A victrola in the far corner softly played a Beethoven symphony.

"Mr. Klein, we're submitting a loan application for Mr. Knobloch, here, for sixteen hundred dollars for 5 years," said Leonard. "With interest, which turns out to be forty-three dollars a month for him. As you will recall he's payin' you thirty-five a month now for rent – he thinks he can conjure up the forty-three."

"Mr. Leonard, five years is a long time – we've got better places to invest our money, and we can get a higher interest rate with it – that's too long," Klein blurted. "And I don't think

Knobloch can afford that monthly payment. He has had a hell-a-va time coming up with thirty-five-dollar-rent over the last four years. He has been late four times – still hasn't paid the late fees. I don't think he can do it."

"I think I can," retorted Walter. "Things are pickin' up in this town – I'm gettin' paintin' and carpentry jobs, and summer's comin' – I'll get plenty of farm work."

"In all due respect, Walter, with the war still goin' on, you are much too optimistic. Believe me, things aren't as rosy as you think. The folks I'm talkin' to in the government say we need to be careful. I'm not goin' to give you the money."

Walter rose from his chair and walked out, leaving Leonard and Klein behind. He stopped off at Baker's R&W to tell him of Klein's decision.

"Klein won't give me the money," said Walter, "so I guess the house is yours if you still want it."

"I tell you what, Knobloch, I'll lend you the money, and I won't charge you any interest – you can make payments on it whenever you can."

"That's mighty generous of you, Baker. "You're goin' to make the missus very happy."

---

Mayor Baker and Klein often met to discuss current issues being considered by the town council as well as those immediately concerning the citizenry at large. With Baker a Democrat and Klein a Republican, their conversations often led to heated discussions of local, state and national politics. Breakfast morning was the most convenient time for them to meet, and they usually met at Emma's Diner. Emma's was the favorite café of most of the rural and town folk and the teenage crowd. Emma bought the restaurant several years ago when the original owner died and she was fending economically for herself after her teacher husband ran off with one of his students, leaving her and the state. She had refurbished the inside with wood façade paneling, Formica-covered tables, Western artwork, and comfortable spring-loaded chairs.

"I can't believe you bailed Knobloch out," said Klein as Emma sloshed coffee into two heavy mugs on the Diner table. "Knobloch dropped the warehouse keys off – told my secretary that he got the money from you, and 'I could shove mine up where the sun doesn't shine'."

"Well, Albert, we've got to help these people in this town out through this mess. Hell, he still owes me eighty-nine dollars for groceries his wife has charged. But I know someday he'll pay it – Knobloch's a good man – those Catholics are honest people."

"Catholic – my butt!" exclaimed Klein. "Those Catholics 'sh__t' in their own nest. All they do is have more and more kids. I swear – all that Knobloch woman has to do is hang her underwear on the bedpost, and she'll have a kid."

# 13

Lara announced one supper evening: "I'm having the Ladies Altar and Rosary Society meet here on Friday afternoon, and I want the house cleaned and the yard 'picked-up'." Raimund, you and Kurt and Konrad take care of the yard – I want all that junk removed, and I want you to rake it. Hanna – you can start inside – Stefan can help and so can Steffi – I'll help too – but I've got some bakin' to do."

"What's the Altar and Rosary Society?" What do they do?" Konrad asked Lara.

"They take care of the altar – you know the linen covering and the small cloths the priest uses to wipe the chalice. They take care of the vestments – clean and iron them. Whenever they meet, they say the Rosary and pray to the Blessed Virgin Mary."

"Ya' know Adele at school sez she thinks we Catholics pray to statues – she goes to Zion Lutheran," said Hanna.

"Hogwash!" said Lara. "The statue is there to remind us of who she is – we ask her to help us to talk to God – that's all it is."

With supper finished and assigning the twins to wash the dishes, Lara put the leftovers into the refrigerator and retired into the dining room to her rocking chair and began to read the Journal Advocate. Although she and Walter had been schooled only to the eighth grade, she was curious and studied the world. She followed the war – her sons Lukas and Kristoff were somewhere in the Pacific – she did not know where – Lukas in the Marines – Kristoff in the Navy. She was disturbed that her German descendants were instigating another war. "What's this world coming to?" she asked herself.

    Finished with reading, Lara moved over to her sewing machine – she resumed the work on two shirts she was making for the twins. Walter was in the living room listening to Gabriel Heater on his Philco – she listened intently to Heater's impassioned deliverance as she pushed the cloth toward the upward and downward moving needle of her Singer. She worked quickly – the start of school was imminent. At ten-thirty and with the news program over, she retired to bed – took out her rosary from under her pillow and prayed for Mary to intercede on behalf of her sons. Walter turned out the lights and followed her to bed.

# 14

Mr. Thomas Trevor announced to his high school English Class, "Your assignment is to write a poem on any topic you choose. Your work is due on my desk two weeks from today." Raimund Knobloch turned in the following composition:

### The Pond

I walk by your shore each day
I'm reminded of your tiny origin
When you were fed only by a spring and rain
Now a river influx fills your belly
It has magnified and swollen your size
Dictating new responsibilities to community
Supplying pursuit of fish and comfort of swim
Each summer your bowels spill out on to the prairie
Sustaining crops of nourishment to animal bodies
And still your brilliant beauty remains
Protected by encirclement of cottonwoods
Your tranquil surface sooths our soul
Reflecting moonlight calming our brain

Raimund Knobloch, 1942

---

Each summer, Klein opened the concession stand on Bubbling Pond. In the summer of 1943, he asked his daughter Heidi to manage it. Klein believed it would be a valuable experience of the business and financial worlds for her. That same summer, Raimund worked at the drugstore. He needed the money to buy school clothes come fall. Raimund swept floors, washed windows, stocked shelves, and worked behind the soda fountain. After closing the stand, Heidi often stopped off at the drugstore on the way home for ice cream treats. Sitting across the fountain bar, she enjoyed Raimund's conversation and banter as he prepared ice cream dishes and sodas and washed dishes. She was discreet and careful not to appear flirtatious. Her father discouraged early dating and made her decline when schoolmates asked her out. More importantly, it must not be known that she was associating often with a Catholic boy. To say it mildly, Albert Klein did not appreciate Catholics. His disdain was widely known all over town. Some wags said it was because his mother, who was Catholic before marrying his German Lutheran father, was physically abused by her father. Others said it was because Catholic boys bullied him as a young boy at school. Nobody knew for sure, but his dislike was readily visible when he was forced to interact with them.

"I went swimming today, Raimund," said Heidi. "The water was warm – had been sitting there for a long time – the sun really heated it up. You ought to come out sometime and try it."

"I swam there many times when I was younger – especially when we lived right on the shore – maybe I'll try it sometime. I'll have to take some time off to do it – I think Mr. Bass will let me off."

"Well, we could swim at night when you're not working," Heidi suggested.

"Excellent idea – let me know when it is a good time for you."

The next week, Raimund agreed to meet Heidi at the boat house at 10 p.m. Both had concealed their suits beneath their street clothes.

"Let's take one of the boats out – we can swim in the middle of the pond – its deeper out there," said Heidi. "Also, maybe we can see where the water bubbles come from – there's a bright moon out tonight – that'll help us find them. They say if you see them, it brings you good luck."

"People say you can't see the bubbles anymore – the pond has too much water in it now – they have too far to go to make it to the surface," said Raimund.

"Well, the pond is down real low now," Heidi volunteered. "They've been irrigating a lot – maybe tonight we'll get to see them."

Approaching mid-pond, Heidi quickly dived off the boat, and Raimund followed. In the shallow depth, their legs and arms were at once wrapped in long strands of elodea, providing for an instant, a feeling of an unescapable stranglehold by a "monster weed." Breaking away, they both arrived at the surface at the same time.

"Boy, that was kinda scary," said Heidi, gasping for air.

"Yal, I thought for a moment that I was a goner," contended Raimund.

They thrashed around in the water for several minutes, sensing the sun-warmed water around their bare-skinned bodies. Raimund climbed into the boat – then grabbed Heidi's arm lifting her aboard.

They sat quietly, saying nothing as they looked over the placid pond surface hoping to see a disturbance – bubbles from the spring below? Were they out there?

"You know, they say the Indians camped here beside Bubbling Pond," said Heidi. "I know that's true because I've found arrowheads in the sand by the concession stand. They say this was a holy place for them."

"Yal, and back then this area was swarming with bison and antelope," said Raimund. "Now all you see is an occasional antelope on the outskirts of town."

They peered into the water, talked, and laughed. They listened to the call of a hooting owl and watched bats intercepting their evening dinner from the warm air above the pond.

"It's peaceful out here," said Raimund. "I can see why the Indians liked this place."

"We better get back," said Heidi. Then with a smirk, she expounded, "If my father finds I'm missing, he'll have me 'whipped in the public square'."

# 15

The high school orchestra program was now in its third year, and twenty-five students were enrolled. Fritz Werner selected Heidi Klein as "first chair." Werner was preparing his students for the Christmas concert – the repertoire included passages from the Messiah and a variety of Christmas carols. He chose Raimund to sing Silent Night.

Raimund saw Heidi every day, and he sat next to her when Mr. Werner lectured. They attended world history class together as well as chemistry and biology. In the cafeteria at noon lunch, they could be seen sitting across from each other. Raimund saw her in the afternoon at the drugstore – sometimes she drank a soda and conversed at the bar – other times she ordered an ice cream cone to eat on her way home and did not stay long. In the evenings they arranged study sessions at the town library – there was a private room they could use if they were preparing for an upcoming test and needed to talk. Word was out all over the school and town that a committed relationship was developing between the two.

Drinking coffee at Emma's Diner one Thursday morning, Mayor Baker remarked to Klein, "I saw you at the concert the other night – what'd you think of it? I thought they performed well."

"I thought so, too," Klein answered. "The program seems to be doing okay – I see their numbers are increasing."

"Heidi's solo playing was flawless – looks like she's getting a lot out it."

"She is – she likes it a lot – I hope she sticks with it all the way into college," said Klein.

"My daughter Sandra has all she can handle with that French horn – I don't how she can get that thing to sound so good – she's so small – I never thought she'd have that much wind in her," said Baker.

"Boy that Knobloch kid can sing! Can't he?" exclaimed Baker.

"Yes, I guess so – for a Catholic – yes – I've never known many Catholics that can sing," said Klein, grinning slightly with his familiar sarcastic response.

"My missus sez he gets his musical talent from his mother – she plays the organ at St. Boniface," said Baker.

"Well, with all those kids of hers, she needs to spend more time at church – she's spent way too much time 'in-the-sack,'" said Klein sarcastically.

"Sandra tells me that things are 'pretty thick' between that kid and Heidi." "What do ya' think about that?" Baker asked.

"I've heard that too – lots of gossip flying around. I don't know if it's true or not. I've never seen the kid around. He's never stepped foot in my house, and what's more, he never will! – I won't stand for it. Sounds like I must have a serious talk with Heidi – things are 'gettin'-outta-hand.'"

# 16

It was mid-November 1943, and Lara had just celebrated her forty-second birthday. At her sewing machine in mid-afternoon, she thought about her life over the last forty years. Where had the time gone? She had been busier than 'a one-armed paper hanger.' Her life had always been that way. Her teenage years on the family farm had been filled with constant activity – cooking, hoeing, canning, milking, gardening, scrubbing, washing, butchering, sewing, needle working and praying. Lara never shied away from physical labor. On the dryland farm with six sisters and one brother, Lara's input was needed. Dryland farming was harsh, and without rainfall for some years, it was tough to make a living. Lara grimaced slightly when the tornado that destroyed their barn one evening came to mind. Her mind began to meander aimlessly. What would have happened if she had gone on to high school instead of ceasing schooling after the eighth grade? If she had gone on to college like her two younger sisters? Lara was stellar in academics – she prided herself that she was "good at mathematics – it was easy for her. At the country grade school, she always won the spelling bee contest. Her father had begun reading to her at an early age, and he checked out books from the Logan County Library in Sterling for her to read. He had taught her to play the organ. In her married life, she had borne twelve children and had placed two into their final resting place. Unlike her two younger sisters who went to college, Lara's life was on a different trajectory – Lara's life was now totally devoted to others, primarily her family. She lived by her father's mantra he constantly recited to them: "We are not born for ourselves."

Lara's Singer sewing motor hummed, and the needle jumped up and down as she fed the cloth underneath it. She thought about Christmas that would be here next month – she had a lot of sewing to do – she was working on pajamas for Walter. Next would be Christmas dresses for twins Katrin and Kerstin – they were five years old now. She had "hitched a ride" with a neighbor lady down the street to Sterling and had bought several yards of cloth from Glass & Bryant's Dry Goods for shirts, skirts, pants, coats, and pajamas that she had planned to make into gifts for her children. She bought underwear, gloves, and socks for the boys, a football, and games (Chinese checkers, playing cards, monopoly) which they would find under the tree Christmas morning – showing Santa had arrived. She would buy oranges, nuts, and candy at Baker's R&W for 'Santa's distribution.' She and Hanna would soon make popcorn balls for inclusion.

She had promised Hanna that she would make a hood for her coat – Hanna's did not have one, and all her schoolmates were buying new coats with hoods – it was the "rage" at school, and Hanna wanted one. "I can probably finish that task with just a couple of hours of work," Lara thought.

Two weeks ago, she and Hanna had made cookies, fudge, and divinity and packed them into boxes for mailing to Lukas and Kristoff. Raimund hauled them to the Post Office in their Radio-Flyer wagon for mailing. Lara mailed them to generic addresses that the military had named – they were vague about their whereabouts – Lara did not know. I hope they get these, Lara wished to herself. She read in the paper that you had to send things six weeks in advance to make sure service members got them before Christmas. She had not seen her sons for over a year. She wondered where they would celebrate Christmas. Was Lukas in some foxhole on a coral island reef somewhere? Was Kristoff on a ship or aircraft carrier? Maybe they were on a military base in Hawaii or some other island?

With money earned at the drugstore, Raimund bought a 6-foot-tall blue spruce at the lumber yard and took it home for the family to decorate. He hung the lights, and his younger siblings followed by carefully placing colored glass balls and tinsel in strategic spots on the sparsely branched tree. He placed the angel icon that Lukas bought three years prior on top, and Hanna arranged the Nativity set of statues on the end table, next to the couch.

For the Knoblochs the Christmas family celebration began on Christmas Eve. Lara always prepared the food – the menu had been set for many years. Her preparation began early on Christmas Eve morning – she mixed up twice as much bread dough as she usually did and set it aside "to rise." She asked Konrad to "sort the beans" which meant removing tiny rocks and dirt particles from the pintos she had selected from the 100-pound sack stored in the pantry. After washing, the beans were placed in a 3-gallon pressure cooker – half-filled with water – along with a portion of diced ham and a bone or two, and Lara's special seasoning of salt and condiments. The cooker lid was screwed on tight, and the liquid mixture was subjected to high heat on the kitchen coal/wood stove. The heat and pressure cooked the beans in a matter of a few hours, creating a thickened brown mixture.

She poured cream from Walter's milk cow into the gallon jar of the churn and instructed Konrad to begin churning. "We've got a lot of cream there, young man, so it may take a while," she said to him, "but we're goin' to need a lot of butter for tonight's supper."

That afternoon, she formed 'balls' of dough, placing them in flat pans and setting them aside to continue 'rising.' They would be popped into the oven right before supper – cooked into 'buns' upon which fresh butter would be smeared, creating bread that went with the savory taste of the bean soup. On a large breadboard, she rolled out dough to a sizeable, flattened piece – placed a mixture of sugar, corn syrup, cinnamon, nutmeg, and butter on it – then rolled it up into a long cylinder, and then sliced it into two-inch rings and placed them on a large cookie-pan – these would be her tasty cinnamon rolls she would serve on Christmas morning.

She took a brief respite to walk to St. Boniface to say her confession to Fr. Gerhardt – Walter and her children had already gone ahead to the church. Kneeling, she began to prepare with the customary 'examination of conscience,' reading in her prayer book the list of sins germane to the common transgressor. She concluded that sins against pride, greed, sloth, and envy were not right for her – definitely, pride and greed did not apply – she was not lazy, and she was not jealous of her neighbor. Perhaps she was eating a little too much in the last several months – at least she noticed she was gaining a little weight. She was a prideful soul, but it had not turned into conceit. She remembered how her mother reminded her when it looked like she was focusing too much on her own self-importance: 'Every bird loves to hear himself sing' – 'be careful – her mother would add.' Lara was not known to gossip – 'I do not have the time,' she said to herself. Her desire was always focused on her husband – no one else ever came to mind – she smiled slightly – thinking that others thought she was lustful because of all of the children she had had. She was confident that God would never punish her for this – in her mind, God had blessed her. She remembered that she had been quick to anger when Kurt and Konrad broke the arm on the couch while playing tackle football in the house – she had swatted them both vigorously – now she regretted her response – Fr. Gerhardt would be hearing about this in her contrition.

With supper over, Hanna washed the dishes and Konrad and Kurt dried them. Now "opening the presents" began. The children had drawn names a month before – each was to receive a gift. Raimund had drawn Hanna's name, and he gave her a sweater he bought in Sterling. He gave Walter a box of cigars – Mr. Bass sold it to him at a reduced price. Lara received a brooch pin – bought at Sterling's Glass and Bryant's. Stefan, drawing Raimund's name, found a used Mozart recording in the antique shop in Sterling – he disguised it by wrapping it in a large box – Raimund was surprised and incredibly pleased – he had bought a phonograph for himself – now he could listen to the beautiful music he had come to know and appreciate.

St. Boniface scheduled two masses for Christmas: one at midnight on Christmas Eve and the other at 9 in the morning on Christmas Day. Lara wanted Raimund to sing a solo at both masses. That night, accompanied by Lara on the organ, Raimund sang:

*Oh Holy Night,*
*The stars are brightly shining*
*It is the night of the dear Savior's birth………*

Raimond's voice resounded with volume and authority as he announced Jesus's birth with the hymn. Lara's fingers pressed forcefully on the keyboard with determination – the twosome's music resonated beautifully in the small church. Raimund's delivery and diction were almost perfect – he had been rehearsing for several weeks under the tutelage of his high school music teacher. It was indeed "a night divine."

The next morning, Lara and Raimund had a repeat performance with the Ave Maria. Lara was pleased – she was proud of her son – if confirmed once again in her mind that Raimund was special – God had supplied him a variety of gifts – he was a fortunate young man. She would continue to do all she could to nourish his talents.

# 17

The school year transitioned into the new year of 1944 with ease – soon it was March and plans for the April Junior-Senior Prom began to solidify. As president of his class, Raimund coordinated all the activities of the prom dance. Since he worked after school, he conducted his committee meetings on Sunday evenings. The class ham-raffle sales had been highly successful, and they now had the resources to make this prom the most successful of any conducted at the high school.

Raimund asked Heidi if she would go with him.

Although not surprised, she hesitated and offered this explanation: "I don't know for sure if I can go – I don't know if I'll be around – my father was planning a family vacation during that time – he wants to spend a week in the Colorado Rockies. Will have to see when he has completed our plans before I can give you a yes."

Raimund waited patiently for her answer – he did not want to press her into a quick decision. He waited and waited – he never reminded her – he never brought the subject up. He never suspected that she might be stalling.

Finally, at the cafeteria, Heidi said to him, "I can't go with you Raimund – my father won't let me – ask somebody else," she said as tears ran down her cheeks. She grabbed his hand across the table and began to weep uncontrollably. She looked at him – she saw hurt and disappointment in his eyes – she saw his astonished, surprised look of unbelievability.

# 18

September 1943

09/1. War is still going on. We heard from Lukas – he's on a ship heading toward a Pacific Ocean island – don't know where. Kristoff is on an aircraft carrier that works out of Pearl Harbor. Heard over the news that some tremendous sea battles are happening with the Japs; he's probably involved. At church, we all pray to God to protect our service members.

09/2. Talked to Heidi only occasionally this summer. She stopped in at the drugstore but didn't seem to want to talk – always in a hurry. Very disappointing; we used to be good friends.

09/3. Hanna decided she did not want to go to college. She found a job as a receptionist in a doctor's office in Sterling. She has moved to an apartment there. I really miss not having her around. My mom cried when Hanna left. I almost did.

09/4. Mom will be working in the school cafeteria when school starts. She says prices for food and clothes are going up, so our family is needing more money. She says she's paying 20% more for coal. She used a lot of it in her kitchen stove this summer with her canning.

09/5. I have saved most of the money I earned at the drugstore this summer. Saturday is my last day of work. I'm going to Schuster's to buy clothes. Need new shoes badly.

09/6. School started today. I took a seat next to Heidi in American History II class. She "gave me the cold shoulder." She was wearing her hair in a ponytail. She is pretty and wears very nice clothes. She had told me once that she and her mother took the train to Denver to shop. She will certainly be voted "The Most-Welled-Dressed."

09/7. They announced at school that we will have student officer elections in two weeks. I'm thinking about running for student body president. I'm looking forward to taking part in my speech class. I think it will help me if I'm elected president.

09/8. My Mom has canned all the stuff out of my dad's garden. People dropped fruits and vegetables off at our house for Mom to can. She and the twins and Steffi canned all summer. Last Sunday I picked apples from Mrs. Schmidt's tree for Mom to can. Mom makes apple sauce. It is my favorite fruit dessert – especially when I eat ginger cookies (that Mom makes) with them. One jar of pumpkin exploded in front of Mom; spreading scalding hot water and hot mush all over her lower neck chest and lower arms. She put butter on her burned skin. Luckily no glass hit her in the face.

09/9. I ordered Mozart's Symphony No. 40 in G Minor from a mail-order house. Mr. Werner recommended this recording. He says it is one of two symphonies written by Mozart in a minor key. He says there is a good movement with the violas. I read in the Journal-Advocate that the Sterling Symphony was going to tackle Mozart's Symphony No. 36 in C major, K. 425, also known as the Linz Symphony. The paper said it was written by Mozart during a stopover in the Austrian town of Linz on his and his wife's way back home to Vienna from Salzburg. It looks like he wrote it in a noticeably brief time; the guy was a genius. I'm going to order tickets for Mom and me.

09/10. No school today. All northeastern Colorado was covered with snow last night, accompanied by wind. Our Logan County was hit hard. I shoveled snow from our sidewalk and from those of our neighbors. Expecting extremely low temperatures tonight. My upstairs bedroom was cold. Snow blew in onto the windowsill. I'm writing this morning at the kitchen table. It is the warmest room in the house.

09/11. Again, no school today. My thoughts are of Heidi. I wrote the following:

## A Musical Friend

I play my clarinet from my position behind afar
Ahead I see her in the violin section as the featured star
I see the back of her head and her long curled hair
I watch as she performs as the orchestra's "first chair"
Her hair waves in synchrony as the bow caresses the strings
In concert an eager audience awaits the sound each stroke brings
At music's end she stands elegantly and then forward bends
Acknowledging their approval that her stellar act lends
The conductor's arm waves appreciatively toward her way
And I marvel at her beauty and enchanting sway

# 19

Northeastern Colorado was subjected to a cold freeze in early September. With later freezes in months following, the ice on Bubbling Pond began to thicken. In December Mayor Baker considered the thickness of the ice was sufficient to sustain the weight and force of humans for skating. His daughter Sandra hosted her senior class at an evening ice-skating party. She asked classmates to supply their shoe sizes if they had no skates – Tom would rent them from Hibbetts Sporting Goods in Sterling. Twenty-seven of the twenty-nine total class members showed up.

Raimund had not been on the ice for a couple of years, so he was intimidated when he first stepped onto the slippery surface. He glided forward and squatted slightly until his knees were bent, and he took a modest wobble. Regaining his stability, he leaned on his left foot, and then with his right, he pushed outward in a diagonal direction; he propelled forward. He repeated this with his right foot first and then with his left. He was getting the "hang of it" again, moving forward and feeling comfortable. As his speed picked up, he felt the cool breeze through his hair and across his chest; it was an enlivening sensation. Soon he was moving in the small circle all his classmates were taking as they hovered closely to the shore. Baker had recommended all not going out too far. It was inevitable that Raimund would take a fall – his body fell with a crash, and he slid past his laughing classmates – flat on his bottom.

With his upper legs tiring, Raimund paused to rest, standing next to the fire Baker had built to stay warm. He saw Heidi, smiling at others as she moved across the ice. She looked natural as if she were meant to be there. Both she and her skates moved fluidly. There was not one jerky movement. She balanced herself so easily; she truly was an expert. She held her arms out at just below shoulder level. Her head was forward, her knees were bent slightly, and her rump elevated. Her strands of long curled hair, reaching from beneath her cap, flowed gracefully in the wind as she moved. She continued to have her body loose throughout the entire time. Heidi was a beautiful, elegant form – like a swan swimming across the water.

It was a clear night with the Milky Way and the surrounding stars readily visible – the bright moonlight glancing off the ice, revealing its slick glassy surface. The limbs of surrounding leafless cottonwoods silhouetted into the sky. The only sounds heard were those of teenager voices and laughter and an occasional barking dog – perhaps startled by a raccoon or a hungry fox. The night temperature was in the upper thirties, but the students stayed warm standing next to the fire. They roasted bratwurst, made hot dogs, and drank hot cider. Donuts or roasted marshmallows were available for dessert.

Raimund saw Heidi standing over the fire – holding a long coat-hangar wire and roasting a marshmallow. He, with wire and marshmallow in hand, stepped up to the fire next to her.

"Good evening, Heidi," he said. "It's been a long time since we've talked. You sure looked good on the ice tonight. How long have you been skatin'?"

"Since I was three. My mother bought me a pair of skates then, and I've been skating ever since. On Saturdays, she would take me to the Galleria in Sterling and let me skate while she was shopping. Been doing it all my life."

"Well, you sure looked good tonight – like a beautiful bird flyin' through the air," said Raimund.

"Thank you, Raimund – that's very kind of you."

Wanting to monopolize her time as much as he could, he at once changed the conversation by asking the question, "Do you know where you're going to go to college next fall? Have you made a final decision?"

"Don't know for sure. I sent off for a lot of information – have received hundreds of brochures. My father thinks I should go to an ivy-league school. I've visited CU and Colorado College – they both are interested in having me attend. My mother and I are going to take a trip to the eastern U.S. and visit some schools. When I get on their campuses, that will help me decide."

"How about you? Have you decided?" she asked.

"No, I haven't – I know it will be someplace in-state – will be the only thing I can afford. CU has a journalism program that is well recognized and interests me."

"You know, I sure miss talkin' to you and havin' you as a good friend," said Raimund.

"Me, too – I miss talkin' to you. But I still think of you as a friend – maybe not a close one – my father won't allow it – and he's not going to change his mind."

Raimund's eyes started to moisten – he had no answer to her situation. He stood motionless and watched his marshmallow wither away with the flames and turn into black smoke.

# 20

Klein High School English teacher, Thomas Trevor, informed Raimund one day after class that Colorado State College of Education was starting a Creative Writing Curriculum Major with an education minor.

"I've looked it over, and I think it's pretty good," said Mr. Trevor. "Also, I know a lot of the instructors there in the English department – they are all good – and they are going to bring in some guest faculty with a journalism background to teach – so they are going to have a good program. The college has a strong internship program with the city newspaper in Greeley – if you could get one of those, it might be an excellent opportunity for you by going to CSCE. You could gain a lot of valuable experience working at The Greeley Tribune – it is one of the best small-town newspapers around."

As the 1944 Spring semester ended, Principal Felix Richter announced the names of the top scholars of the senior class. Heidi Klein was named valedictorian, and Raimund Knobloch was appointed salutatorian. At the graduation exercise, the orchestra played the Pomp and Circumstance March as the senior class entered the gym and onto the stage. Accompanied by the orchestra, Raimund sang the National Anthem as the proceeding began and God Bless America at the finish. Heidi played a Vaughan Williams violin concerto: The Lark Ascending. Both Heidi and Raimund presented speeches to the class and the audience.

"Thanks, Emma," said Mayor Baker as Emma poured hot coffee into a cup set in front of him at the Diner.

"My pleasure, Tom," said Emma. "Where's your sidekick? I haven't seen him around for a while."

"He'll be here – just talked to him on the phone – he's been in Denver – the Legislature was meetin' and it has adjourned. I'm anxious to find out how the session went. That water legislation they passed is going to affect Klein's water costs. I wanna find out what he thinks about it."

Suddenly, the outside door opened, and Albert Klein entered. He sat down across the table from Tom, and Emma poured a cup of coffee for him.

"I understand you've been in Denver legislatin'," said Emma.

"Yes, I been hagglin' with those goddamn Democrats over water rights. They are the most stubborn bastards that I've ever seen. They're always wanting the government to do something for them – they need to get off their butts and start working."

"How've you been, Tom? It's been six weeks since I saw you at graduation."

"Gettin' along fine – sent my first check over to Boulder to pay for Sandra's room and board for her first semester – cost me three hundred and forty-five dollars – that's just for the first quarter."

"What's she taking over there?" Klein asked.

"Biology – she's in the pre-med program – wants to be a pediatrician."

"How about Heidi? With her grades and being valedictorian, she could get into any institution in the country."

"She's going to Wellesley – that's where her mother went – I couldn't get her interested in Harvard."

"I thought she and Raimund Knobloch gave really good speeches," said Baker.

"I wonder what jerk-water college that Knobloch kid is going to?" asked Klein.

"Colorado State College of Education in Greeley," Baker answered. "That's where Sandra said he was going. I guess he wants to be a writer – goin' to minor in education."

"Well with that degree he'll never amount to anything – he'll be poor all of his life – especially if he ends up teaching."

"That kid's pretty talented – who knows – he may write a best-selling novel and make a lot of money," said Baker.

"Fat chance that happening," barked Klein.

# 21

Raimund hitched a ride with Günther Bernhardt, his high school classmate, to Greeley to search for an apartment for his stay at CSCE. Günther was going to live in the dormitory, but Raimund opted for an apartment. It would be cheaper, and he wanted to do his own cooking. He found a one-roomer with an attached kitchenette, found above Campus Pharmacy on $8^{th}$ Avenue – right across from the college. It was serendipitous – the place was vacant because the graduate student who had occupied it for a couple of years had just moved out. The location was ideal being close to campus, and with a Piggly Wiggly grocery store two blocks away and St. Peter's Catholic Church four blocks off, all his basic needs were met.

Being salutatorian of his high school class, Raimund had been granted a tuition-waiver scholarship, available to scholar students attending a state institution. In addition, based on his SAT scores, the English Department awarded him with their prestigious James Michener scholarship, named after the author who had taught at the college, and awarded to a promising first-year student enrolled in the creative writing program. He walked to Ross Hall to visit with his English advisor about the courses he would be taking in the first quarter. He stopped off at Frazier Hall, home of the music department. High school music teacher, Fritz Werner, had suggested he visit with the director of the Choral-Aires – a student choral group. "With your voice and singing experience, I think you'd easily qualify for acceptance into the group," said Werner. Raimund scheduled an audition for when he was back on campus for the fall quarter.

It was four o'clock in the afternoon when he walked six blocks further down 8$^{th}$ Avenue to the offices of *The Greeley Tribune* where he met with the night editor. Raimund had visited with his high school English teacher, Thomas Trevor, a month ago in the drugstore, where Trevor informed him:

"I talked to Marcus Neubauer, the night editor at the *Tribune*. He said for you to stop and see him when you get to Greeley. He wants to interview you. He sez they have a couple of internships available that pay well."

Raimund filled out the application and spent an hour talking with Neubauer. He left the Tribune feeling confident that he would be invited into the program – he desperately needed the financial support it provided.

On the drive back to Klein, Raimund remarked to Günther, "If I get the internship, I'll have enough money to stay in school for the whole year – it, with what I saved up from workin' this summer, should be enough to support me."

"How many hours do you work at the newspaper? Günther asked.

"Twenty. Working on weekends – I can handle it."

---

On the first day of fall quarter with all the creative writing majors assembled in one classroom, the Head of the Department of English, Austin Blough, explained the new creative writing program at CSCE.

"The program is unique in that it combines intensive writing workshops with seminars that study literature from a writer's perspective," Blough stated. "While you students develop and hone your own literary technique in workshops, the creative writing seminars explore literary technique and history, exposing you to the various ways that language has been used to make writing an art."

Blough turned his back to them and wrote the words writing workshop on the chalkboard. Turning back to face them he then emphasized its description, "The writing workshop is the core element in the practice of creative writing. In the workshop, you will produce original works of fiction, poetry, or nonfiction, and give them to your classmates and professor for a close critical analysis. The workshop critiques will assess the mechanics and merits of your piece of writing, while individual conferences with your professors will distill the various critiques into a direct plan of action to improve your work. Therefore, as a creative writer, you will develop by practicing the craft under the diligent critical attention of your peers and your professors."

He paused for a moment and looked around at twenty or more students, confirming in his mind that they understood, then he wrote the word seminar on the board and continued – saying: "The seminar is the second important part of the creative writing program. The seminar provides the intellectual foundation that informs you and deepens your work. You will read a book each week and engage in table discussions about the artistic attributes of that book."

Holding three fingers up, Blough stated, "The 'third leg' of your education in creative writing will be drawn from various courses that are offered by our distinguished faculty in the Department of English." Then he wrote the word coursework on the board.

"And thus, ladies and gentlemen, we have a three-pronged approach to your creative writing education here," said Blough. "Through workshops, seminars, and coursework, you will develop your craft. You will be mentored and guided by our expert faculty. Welcome to our program. All of us here on the staff wish you the very best."

Raimund met with his advisor and enrolled in the workshop and seminar and in the introductory courses: ENG 1001 - Writing, Reading, & Culture and ENG 1201 - Introduction to American Literature, each at 4 hours credit for a combined total of 16 hours. He was accepted into the Choral-Aires for which he would receive 1 hour of credit.

Raimund was aware his first quarter in college would be the most challenging time of his life – coupled with work, a lot would be expected of him. However, Raimund knew his enrollment in this creative writing program was one of the greatest opportunities of his life. He knew he was most fortunate – he vowed to himself not to 'screw it up.' He wanted his mother to be proud of his accomplishments."

# 22

Raimund walked six blocks down 8th Ave. and entered through the double doors of The Tribune building. It was Tuesday afternoon, and he had just finished listening to the lecture in his *American Literature* class. Inside, he asked the receptionist if he could see Mr. Neubauer. She indicated he was visiting with the chief editor for the moment and requested for him to take a seat.

Raimund surveyed the vast array of office cubicles spread over a large room of perhaps 600 square feet. He could hear several conversations that were taking place among staffers, some on the phone, all amongst the ratta-tat sound of busy typewriters. He saw black and white photos of governors, mayors, chamber presidents, city and college events, students, and dignitaries, hanging on the brown brick wall next to where he sat. The publisher, identified by a large block letter sign over his door, was isolated in a glass-walled office talking on the phone. Smartly dressed women in high heels walked through the office maze carrying memos, writings, and papers to individuals holed-up in their small spaces. The activity enthralled Raimund. He sensed right away the importance of the production all were participating in to create. He was glad he would have the opportunity to see this operation and contribute to its success.

Neubauer finished his meeting, and seeing Raimund through the glass walls of his office, he beckoned him to come in.

"How was your summer?" he asked as Raimund sat down in the high-backed leather chair in front of his desk.

"Very productive, sir. I had a good payin' job, and I managed to save my earnings in preparation for college. With them and with my earnings here, I'm confident I'll have enough money to keep me in school."

"Very good – Raimund. I hear from the English department head you received some scholarship money as well."

"Yes, they're helpin' a lot with payin' tuition and fees," Raimund responded.

"To start you out, we've scheduled you to visit with each member of our staff and have them explain what they do," said Neubauer. "I'm going first, so I'll tell you what goes on with me as night editor."

"Sounds good," said Raimund as he reached into his backpack for a tablet and pencil, wanting to take notes.

"I came into this job with several years of journalist experience and a set of journalism skills. I have a keen understanding of news writing and story structure. I graduated from the University of Missouri with a degree in journalism. There, I obtained a strong background in English language fluency and copy-editing skills. I'm bilingual with Spanish fluency, which is helpful in communicating with our Hispanic population in this area. In this job, you have to pay attention to detail and work to tight deadlines with a quick turnaround."

"Being the night editor, Mr. Neubauer, when does your workday start?" asked Raimund.

"I start at 2pm and work until 10pm – five days a week – Monday through Friday. I have responsibility for the final layout of the news pages and writing headlines and photo captions. I proofread and edit. Occasionally on my watch, an important news event occurs, and I have to mobilize reporters to the scene and get on the phone to obtain details. On these occasions, I usually must work overtime until we get the final story."

"I guess there are times when your job can be overwhelming, aren't there?" exclaimed Raimund.

"Right, but I like what I do – I would not want to do anything else. Seein' that printed copy each day with all the pertinent news is very satisfying."

"Do you think I could help out with the reporting sometime?" Raimund asked.

"I think you can – we'll have you 'shadow' a reporter first, so you can get the hang of it. We'll probably have you doing other things as well – you know when workers are absent."

Neubauer leaned forward in his seat and said, "Matter of fact, there is a substitute job today where you can help us out. Our night custodian is ill – we're thinking you can take his place by sweeping the floors and dumping out the trash cans. This will help us out a lot if you can do this."

"That I can do. I've done it many times at the drugstore where I used to work." Suddenly, the stark reality of the 'real world' was firmly set in Raimund's consciousness. In all professions, sometimes one must start at the bottom.

# 23

March 1944

3/1. Went to the Music Library and checked out Mozart's Symphony 38 in D Major – also referred to as the Prague Symphony. It only has 3 movements, compared to the traditional 4. I play Mozart as background when I'm studying.

3/2. Spring quarter begins on March 4th. Will be taking physical science (required) and a poetry class.

3/3. The state high school basketball tournament is coming up – Mr. Neubauer has assigned me and a Tribune reporter to cover the three-day event. I'm covering the Class C playoffs. Will miss two days of classes – will get lecture notes from friends.

3/4. Got my grades for the winter quarter. All A's. I made the Dean's List for the fall quarter – again all A's. Started attending classes today. Got my first assignment in poetry class: Write a poem on any subject we want.

3/5. Mr. Neubauer critiqued and edited the basketball articles I had written. He submitted them for printing and listed me as the author. I was thrilled when I saw my name in print.

3/6. Choral-Aires will be presenting a concert to CSCE students in Gunter Hall. The director says he wants me to sing a solo. Will be deciding on the song selection real soon. Have invited Mom to attend. Hanna has her own car. She will bring Mom.

3/7. I attended the Sweetheart Ball with Sara Belichick. She is in my poetry class. She accepted my invitation. Gave her a carnation corsage they were selling on campus. The band was excellent. She had to teach me to dance. I had never been to a dance in high school.

3/8. Bought a 5-pound sack of pintos at Piggly Wiggly. I cooked one-half of them. I added bacon and let the mixture simmer on the stove all day. Studied while they cooked. Ate them for supper along with sliced bread and butter and milk.

3/9. Attended 8 am mass at St. Peter's. They have a good choir. Priest gave a nice homily on the need to read Scripture. Must try to read more of it myself. Had pintos for lunch and supper. Spent the day studying.

3/10. I met Günther at Bru-Inn after class. We drank cokes as we talked about our own respective future plans. He's majoring in business administration. He says he wants to start his own business when he graduates. Thinks his dad will help him get started. Got me thinking that I should start my own newspaper. That would be a business where I'd be using my degree.

3/11. In several sessions, Mr. Neubauer explained the AP Style of writing to me. It is a usage guide provided by the Associated Press and used by The Tribune. He gave me an AP Style manual to read and to keep as a reference.

3/12. To provide experience in editing, Mr. Neubauer gave me several articles to review and to correct errors in grammar, punctuation, and spelling. He also wanted me to verify the factual correctness of the information. I had to make several phone calls. He encouraged me to rewrite the text if I thought it would improve clarity and readability.

3/13. As I take part in copy-editing exercises, I'm reminded of the "five C's" I learned in one of my classes: making the article <u>c</u>lear, <u>c</u>orrect, <u>c</u>oncise, <u>c</u>omprehensible, and <u>c</u>onsistent.

3/14. I read a few Bible chapters written by Luke – I like Luke – he was a learned man, and approaches things with an historical perspective.

3/15. This is a draft of my poem to be submitted as a requirement in my poetry class:

## Widow Schumacher

It's morning – twenty minutes after eight

I walk to school, five blocks from my house

I see the mist of my breath passing my face

Uncleared sidewalks are covered with evening fallen snow

I walk on the street, following a tire path left in the white powder

Widow Schumacher is sweeping clear a path from the street to her door

She recognizes me

I was the one who delivered groceries from Baker's R&W to her

the morning after the blizzard two weeks ago

She waves to me as I pass by

I recall last summer delivering the lower legs and toes of four chickens

Wrapped in layered pages of the Journal-Advocate

Discards from my mother's butchering that our family would not eat

But knowing Mrs. Schumacher would make a delectable soup

Salvaging a scarce meat source from the appendages of fowl

# 24

It was summer and Bubbling Pond was bustling with activity. Fishermen in rented boats were reeling in sunfish and crappie and perch, and sunbathers lay on blankets and towels on white sand near shore, soaking up the warm rays of the afternoon sun. Others were seated at the bar of the concession stand, eating hamburgers and hot dogs and drinking Nehi sodas. A couple of children, standing on the dock with cane poles with hooked lines immersed, were hoping, and patiently waiting for an unwary fish to swallow the delectable worm they offered. The argumentative, boisterous voices of several teenage boys playing volleyball resonated over the water. A family of domesticated ducks moved under the dock and paddled single file out to the deeper water. A blue heron, hidden behind a fallen tree trunk, probed the shallow water for a meal of minnows. Tall cottonwoods, surrounding The Pond and fortified by the readily available water, displayed their fluttering leaves in glorious green splendor. Their canopy tops of barren, leafless branches were a reminder of the repeated cold freezes the Klein region experienced in the previous months. New growth of sedges and cattails bordered the shore on the far side of the pond, and hidden, rooted stems of elodea spread over the pond bottom; they had elongated into three-foot long, tiny cylinders encircled with small leaves, reaching upward to capture the diluted sunlight. To sustain the irrigation needs of surrounding farms, Bubbling Pond was kept full, and a small trickle of water flowed over the spillway.

Raimund had sublet his Greeley apartment to a summer-school graduate student for June, July, and August, and he moved back to his Klein home for the summer. He resumed his part-time job at Bass's Drug and his participation in the church choir. He shared a bedroom with the twins – they were in bunk beds and he was in a single bed. The twins soon learned they would be subjected to listening to Mozart each night when Raimund retired. Lara was ecstatic that Raimund was home again, and prepared his favorite foods: pinto bean soup, bratwurst and cabbage, chicken soup with her homemade noodles, and banana cream pie. She willingly washed the backlog of dirty clothes he had accumulated over the past several months. She marveled at how his singing voice had matured, and how his choral experience at college had improved his tone and delivery. She basked in the glory she learned when Raimund shared with her that he had received all A's for each of the three-quarters of his academic endeavors at CSCE. She kept her pride to herself, expressing it only to Walter, but never to Raimund. She was not one to shower any of her children with praise – she had not received it from her parents, and her children would not either. She perceived that praise extolled on one at the expense of another could fragment family cohesiveness. Nevertheless, she recognized Raimund was unique – he had been blessed with a myriad of special talents. She was certain he was destined to have a successful life – no matter what he chose to do. She took solace in the confidence she felt that Raimund was well on his way.

---

 Heidi was back in Klein as well, having finished one year at Wellesley. Her father had obtained a job for her at Schuster's. Albert Klein rationalized that she could get more business experience at the department store, not available to her when managing the concession stand at The Pond. They assigned her to work in the cosmetics section. One afternoon, she walked down to the drugstore during her break. Raimund prepared the chocolate malt she ordered.

 "It's good to see you, Heidi. "It's been almost a year since we've seen each other."

"Yes, it has. It's good to see you as well. How did things go at Greeley?" she asked.

"I had a good year – managed to finish it without owing anybody – I had an excellent job at The Tribune. They let me do some reporting. I covered some high school sports – I covered the state basketball tournament. It was a wonderful experience. I work closely with the night editor at the paper – I'm learning a lot – kinda makes me want to work in the business using my writing skills. How about you? How was it in Massachusetts?"

"Well, it was cold there – I joined the ski club – had never skied here in Colorado. I lived in the dorm – made a lot of friends – I spent a lot of time studying – they have so many requirements. I joined the art and music society – we went to Boston to visit the museums and to attend symphony concerts. I played in the student symphony. My father wants me to have a business background, so I'm majoring in economics – I like it, and I'm doing very well in it."

"Did you interact with the guys at Harvard or MIT? I hear that they invade Wellesley on the weekends and prey on you beautiful, naive damsels."

"Yes, I hooked up with Herschel Wenzel from Harvard – you remember him, don't you?" He graduated with us here in Klein – his dad owns Wenzel Realty over on First Avenue. He's studying architecture."

"Yes – I remember him – a smart guy – he just didn't work very hard."

"He goes to our church – he's home here now for the summer," said Heidi.

"Well, I gotta go, Heidi – gotta get some shelves stocked before I go home. You can pay Mr. Bass at the cash register on your way out."

"Bye Raimund – have a good summer."

Raimund noted that Heidi was more beautiful than ever before. She was using beauty products that enhanced and smoothed her complexion – her lips, a bright ruby-red, were enticing and appealing. Her curled hair now had streaks of blonde, each curl neatly in place, evidence of a recent trip to the hairdresser. Her long necklace bore a Wellesley medallion draped down over her sweater between her prominent breasts. From a distance, he watched intently as she walked to the door. Raimund realized she was no longer a girl, but was now a mature, beautiful woman and a sophisticated one to behold.

# 25

Lara lay in bed with a rosary clasped in one hand. She was giving thanks to the Lord. Her two sons appeared from the War unscathed. Lukas, now a career Marine, was stationed at Quantico, VA, undergoing officer's training. Kristoff, discharged from the Navy, was working in New York City as a salesperson for an Italian import company. Both, traveling from California by train, had stopped off at Klein to spend their annual leave with their Knobloch family. Lukas was home for Thanksgiving, and Kristoff spent Christmas with the family. Lara thanked God profusely for guiding them to safety these last four years. She thought how grateful she was that "the war" was over. She was full of optimism – folks were saying that the economy would be picking up – she liked her job at the school cafeteria, and Walter was getting plenty of opportunities to work.

In June, Walter presented Lara with an electric clothes washer – it was used, but it was a welcome asset in reducing her labor in the weekly chore of washing the clothes of her large family. Before, she had scrubbed clothes on a washboard – now the back-and-forth motion of the central agitator did the cleaning for her. Before, she had hand-cranked each item between the rubber cylinders of her mechanical washer, now she simply fed them through the electric-propelled rollers. She could always depend upon the help of Kurt and Konrad to hang the washed articles on the outside clothesline.

Walter had planted the traditional garden, and Lara had already begun canning the harvestable produce. Walter left a space in the garden front, facing the house, for Lara to plant flowers. Lara planted cosmos, a flowering annual, from a seed packet she bought at Baker's R&W. The long slender stems had produced pink flowers that looked like daisies that attracted bees, butterflies, and even birds. Lara discovered she could induce secondary flowering by removing dead flowers. She hoped to have a flowering cosmos all summer long. She was amazed at how little maintenance they needed. She was proud of the added beauty the large flowering grove brought to her garden and front yard. She salvaged seeds from the base of withering flowers and stored them for planting next spring.

In September, Lara resumed her cafeteria job at the school. When there was excess food left over, her boss encouraged her to take it home and serve her family. The twins, Konrad and Kurt, were promising athletes and played on the Klein High School football team. Konrad was quarterback, tossing passes to wide receiver Kurt and carrying the ball for needed yardage and into the end zone on many occasions. Lara attended home games, played on Friday afternoons. She had become a real student of the game of football and enticed Hanna to take her to some away games. Walter attended the games whenever he could get off work.

# 26

As his junior year approached at CSCE, Raimund found himself totally immersed in the operations of a newspaper. He looked forward to the one-on-one conversations with editor Neubauer when they took an evening break at supper time. Eating their bagged meal, Raimund shared his academic and learning experiences with Neubauer, and Neubauer in turn talked about his endeavors at prior newspaper jobs, his university education, his philosophy as editor, his interaction with townspeople, the ongoing internal events and challenges at The Tribune, the business side of newspapering, and a variety of newspaper related topics. Raimund came away from these conversations realizing that interpersonal communication skills were a key part of success in the newspaper world. It was a world of creativity, a world in which he was beginning to feel quite comfortable.

Raimund worked with staffers in arranging page layouts of photos, articles, and advertisements. He worked with reporters who assigned him to check and verify the facts of their stories, using the phone and searching other print media. He made sure that dates and statistics were correct. He shadowed local reporters, listening and taking notes, and aided in the writing of their submissions. On occasion he made trips to the college library, checking out reference books that staffers needed in their research. One of his primary, routine tasks was keeping the order of the archive collection of past editions; these were searched constantly by staffers and required careful cataloging in their correct sequence. In addition, he was asked to keep the orderliness and cleanliness of the break room, requiring frequent washing of dishes, and sweeping the floor.

After several information meetings with The Tribune publisher, Raimund realized the importance of business management in a newspaper operation. He casually mentioned to Günther, "I may want to start my own newspaper someday, but I don't have any business background." To which Günther responded, "You may want to take a course about starting up a business – our business school offers one – you might want to take it."

"Perhaps next year as an elective," said Raimund. "Right now, I'm crammed full with required coursework."

Because he was fascinated with newspapers, Raimund decided the education minor was no longer the option he wanted to pursue. He concluded more background in literature would be more proper for him as a creative writer, and he enrolled in ENG 2601 – An Introduction to Shakespeare. He also enrolled in the fall quarter seminar where writers are provided a chance to read their work to the patrons of the Writer's Pen Bar & Grill on the south end of 8th Avenue near LaSalle.

"The readings take place in the evening on the last Thursday of every month," said Mathew Donohue, his advisor. "We feature fiction, non-fiction, poetry, and dramatic readings from a wide range of authors, both in the college as well as out, both established and beginning writers, and resident as well as visiting authors. I hear some of your work is pretty good – we schedule two to three writers a month – you may want to take part."

# 27

When the '45 Christmas season arrived in Klein, it was met with snow and low temperatures. As usual, Bubbling Pond was frozen over, and merry-making skaters, young and old, cheeks red from the cold, glided gleefully over the ice. With wooden-crate goals and sticks carved out of plywood, a group of boys carried out a semblance of a hockey game by sliding and hitting a small wood block across the icy pond. A bearded old-timer, keeping warm with a stocking cap on his head and a scarf around his neck, was standing on the dock and feeding corn to a family of ducks waddling on the ice. Leaf-barren cottonwoods stood motionless near shore, their long slim limbs reaching into the bright sunlit sky.

Downtown, large mounds of cleared snow lay along the streets. Lamp posts were wrapped with garlands of holly, and wreaths were mounted on business doors. The traditional tall ponderosa, the hallmark of the Klein Christmas panorama, was decorated with hundreds of lights and was placed in the intersection of Main Street and $10^{th}$ Avenue, forcing drivers to swerve their cars around it as the heavy Christmas traffic moved slowly along.

Vertical and horizontal strands of lights bordered the perimeter and inner contours of the First National Bank; a lighted Christmas tree stood majestically on the top of the stairs leading to the building entrance. A lifelike Nativity scene was displayed in front of the Zion Lutheran Church, and a churchyard blue spruce sparkled with blinking white lights. Through the window of Schuster's Department Store, shoppers viewed a miniature sleigh with Santa and his reindeer suspended above a snow-covered landscape; inside, parents were in line with their children, anxiously awaiting a sojourn with Santa Claus. Bass Drugs was giving miniature candy canes to all patrons; outside its door, a Salvation Army Santa Claus stood, ringing a bell, asking for contributions. Expecting a late rush of shoppers, shelves of Baker's R&W featured added sources and amounts of hazelnuts, pecans, Brazil nuts, hard candy, and boxes of chocolates; a stack of ten 5-pound hams was stored in his refrigerated showcase.

Lara was especially joyful this Christmas. For the first time in many years, all her children would be coming home. Kurt and Konrad had completed their first semester at Colorado University and were home on Dec 18$^{th}$. Lukas, recently promoted to the rank of Captain in the Marines, was granted a 30-day leave; he was traveling to Klein via train. Kristoff was flying into Denver from New York and was taking the bus to Klein. Both Lukas and Kristoff were scheduled to arrive on the 23$^{rd}$. Raimund arrived on the 21$^{st}$, and Hannah was to drive in from Sterling on Christmas Eve. To accommodate these five guests with sleeping arrangements, the younger siblings moved to other bedrooms where Walter assembled cots brought down from the attic. Kristoff's gifts had already arrived and were placed under the tree; they were lavish and wrapped elegantly – he had shopped at New York's Macy's and Saks Fifth Avenue. For two days Steffi, Stefan, Kerstin, and Katrin cleaned the whole house thoroughly, dusting furniture and washing windows, scrubbing, and waxing linoleum-covered floors.

Lara was up early on Christmas Eve morning – she had a lot of food preparation to do. She concocted a large pan of bread dough and rolled-up handful-balls for buns she would serve with the pinto bean soup she had started in a 3-gallon pressure cooker. She baked several pans of cinnamon rolls and 6 loaves of bread, to be served for breakfast on Christmas morning. She assigned Steffi to churn cream for fresh butter. Stefan sustained fuel supplies of wood and coal in buckets placed near the kitchen stove. Lara baked four banana-cream pies for the next day's Christmas dinner. That evening, Walter, Lara and their ten children sat down for their traditional supper meal. Walter said the blessing, and then Kristoff set out wine glasses for Lara, Lukas, Hanna, Walter, and himself; he had brought home a bottle of Italian wine. All the others were drinking milk, amply provided by Walter's cow. They raised their glasses upward as Kristoff toasted Lara and Walter; he then gave praise to the Christ Child.

---

As music director, Lara scheduled a rehearsal of the choir at St. Boniface on the evening of Dec 22$^{nd}$. Featured with solo parts, Raimund sang O' Holy Night with them at Midnight Mass and the Ave Maria on Christmas Day. The twins, Kirsten and Katryn, now 10 years old, were bona fide choir members and were joined by Hanna. The Ladies Altar and Rosary Society had decorated the inside of St. Boniface with greenery and poinsettias. Father Gerhard brought out two gold candelabras from storage and placed them on tables on each side of the altar. A small Nativity display was in front of the altar, and a wreath hung in front of the pulpit. Fr. Gerhard read Luke's Gospel, narrating the Lord's birth. Throughout the Mass, parishioners listened intently as the music resonated from the choir loft; at Mass end, Fr. Gerhard asked them to join in singing Silent Night.

---

On Christmas morning Heidi Klein and three of her former high school orchestra schoolmates were assembled as a stringed quartet, to perform the *Hallelujah Chorus* from Handel's Messiah at Zion Lutheran Church. Heidi, a violinist, two violists, and a cellist had rehearsed all week under the guidance and leadership of the church music director. The church was packed with faithful churchgoers, curious to see their home-grown members perform and listen to their talented choir sing carols. The sanctuary was laced with fifty or so potted poinsettias, and small wreaths clung to the pews along both sides of the wide center aisle. The iconic, twisting wooden staircase, ascending to the raised pulpit, was adorned with greenery and small white lights. Flickering candles on the windowsills supplied the only light to the seated audience, but bright spotlights pinpointed the quartet, the choir, and the pulpit.

After the performance, Heidi rode home with Herschel Wenzel, son of Klein realtor Harvey Wenzel. Herschel, attending Harvard, was home for the holidays. Back in Massachusetts, he and Heidi had been seeing each other often over the past year.

# 28

"Well, we finally graduated!" Günther exclaimed as he raised his coke glass to his lips. "Yes – it's hard to believe – time has gone by fast – it seems like yesterday when four years ago, you and I drove over here to nail-down our places to live," said Raimund.

"Did your parents come to the graduation?" Raimund asked.

"They did – so did my grandmother and my sister. My aunt and uncle from Denver also came. How about you?"

"My parents came – my sister Hanna was there – as well as all my younger brothers and sisters. My high school English teacher attended. He was surprised and pleased when I told him what I was going to do. My boss from The Tribune – Neubauer was there – he gave me this Elgin watch," said Raimund as he raised his wrist for Gunther to see. "It's a good one – will last me a lifetime."

Raimund looked around and noted that Bru-Inn was empty – spring quarter was over – students had gone home, and summer school had not started. He and Günther had met in this campus hangout many times. It was there where they discussed and formulated their plans. They were joining in with a business venture.

"Have you given any more thought to the name of it?" Raimund asked.

"I like the sound of 'The Klein Courier.' The word 'courier' conveys a meaning of 'carrying a message.' I think that's cool."

"What do you think of the idea of changing the 'C' to 'K' like we talked about?" Raimund asked.

"I like that, too. It's another way of grabbing people's attention."

"By the way, my dad said he would loan us money. He said if we need it, he will co-sign a note with me if I wanted to take a loan from Klein First National," said Günther. "How about you?"

"I could never get a loan from Klein First National – Ole man Klein just won't let it happen – he turned my dad down – I'm sure he wouldn't let me in the door. I talked to Mayor Baker over spring break, asking him about what I could do. He said for me to come and see him – he thought I could get a loan from a bank in Sterling – he said he would co-sign with me. He is excited – thinks the paper will be good for the town – and thinks the businesses will support it. He liked the idea of us starting out first as a monthly – he appreciated our caution."

"We'll need to draw-up a business plan," Günther stated. "I've started on it. I'll give it to you so you can supply your input. I guess it makes sense to list you as the editor and me as the business manager. Doesn't it?"

"Sure does," exclaimed Raimund. "Mayor Baker said he would advertise in it – we can make him our first customer."

"You know, the other day I was talkin' to my dad about the paper," said Gunther, "and he came up with a witty remark."

"Oh yeah, what did he say?" asked Raimund.

"He said it would be great to have The Kourier layin' on the floor of every toilet in town. And then I said to him, 'let's hope that happens'."

Raimund smiled. He knew he and his partner were well-prepared to face the future.

# 29

Heidi, now a college graduate and uncertain about her future, returned to Klein to spend the summer. Schuster's invited her back to work in the cosmetics department, but instead she chose women's fashions. She is now dressed in the latest styles featured in fashion magazines, bought from Denver boutiques frequented by her mother and her. Traveling to Denver by train, they stayed overnight at the Brown Palace Hotel. Dressed in the finest, Heidi's hourglass figure was always accented with high waist tops, padded or ruffled shoulders, and A-line skirts, accompanied by high heels. Her workplace attire usually consisted of knee-length, rayon dresses, pleated and buttoned up front, cinched at the waist with a belt, and ruffled shoulders. Other times, she wore blouses and sweaters paired with pleated wool skirts. She kept her hair long, draped with giant, swirling curls. When attending church, she wore a felt fedora with wrist-length, matching-color gloves. Wherever she went in Klein, her appearance gave her celebrity status.

Mayor Baker co-signed for Raimund's loan from Sterling's Logan County Bank. He allocated a one-bedroom apartment in one of his complexes to Raimund – he admitted him with no deposit and charged him one-half the normal monthly rent. He leased a small office space to the newspaper on the third floor of his office building on Main Street and arranged for two desks and two chairs to be placed in it. Raimund and Günther had access to the office either by elevator or stairs, and they viewed Main Street below through a large window. Baker gave them the first six months free.

"What's the status of your printing presses?" Baker asked.

"We bought them second-hand from a newspaper in Nebraska. They should arrive by truck next week."

"Well, if you need to, you can store them in the basement of this building until you figure out where you want them permanently. Matter of fact you can put them there in the basement if you want to. I won't charge you any rent for the first year."

"That is mighty generous of you, Mr. Baker. We may take you up on it. You have been magnanimous already."

"I wanna help. I want you boys to be successful. It will be great for Klein."

Raimund and Günther met with the Chamber of Commerce and the Kiwanis and Lions Clubs, telling them of their plans. Albert Klein was a member of the CofC Board. He had reluctantly approved a loan to Günther. He expressed his skepticism, "I don't think you have the readership here, gentlemen, that you think you have."

"We've conducted our survey, Mr. Klein," said Günther. "The citizens and business owners have said they are ready for it, and they will support it. Mayor Baker has shared the population data of the town with us. The projections are that Klein will continue to grow at a rate of 4 percent per year over the next decade."

"Remember too, Mr. Klein, this is going to be both an urban and a rural newspaper," Raimund interjected. "There's a lot of farm families out there who will subscribe. We'll keep them engaged with articles that are informative and entertaining. Our survey shows that most of them are educated, and they want this sort of thing. The Klein Kourier will be on their coffee tables along with the Saturday Evening Post and the Reader's Digest."

―――――――――――

Raimund entered through the revolving door of Schuster's – he had an appointment with the business manager to place an ad in The Kourier. He traversed across the wide aisle through Women's Wear on his way to the business office in the back of the store. From the corner of his eye, he noticed Heidi stooped over and sorting through a rack of hanging skirts. She did not see him as he approached.

"Hello Heidi," Raimund blurted out.

Heidi looked up and turned abruptly, surprised to see who was in front of her. She at once grabbed him and gave him an energetic hug. Raimund was unprepared – he was not expecting this. He instinctively reciprocated by wrapping both of his arms around her. Raimund's memory instantly shifted to the days of high school – the visits in the cafeteria and the library – the swim in Bubbling Pond.

"My gosh, Raimund, what brings you in here?"

"I'm meeting with your business manager. I want him to buy an ad in our newspaper."

"Yes, I heard what you and Günther are doing from my father. How's it going?"

"We're just getting started. We're trying to get the first edition out sometime in December – right before Christmas."

"What's up with you?" Raimund queried.

"I'm just biding my time until I decide what I want to do. I'm starting to like it here. I've been going to shows in Denver and Omaha with the buyer – the fashion industry is fascinating."

"Well, you certainly are well-dressed for the part," said Raimund. "You look very pretty."

"Thank you, Raimund. That's very nice of you. You've always been very gracious."

# 30

"Good morning Raimund," said Emma. "Somebody told me you were back in town. What's goin' on?"

"I'm here for good. I'm starting up a newspaper here. I'm doing it with Günther Bernhardt. You remember him, don't you?"

"I sure do. You guys used to come in here all the time when you were in high school. I heard you went to school over in Greeley."

"I did and so did Günther. We graduated last May."

Emma placed a cup of coffee in front of Raimund and then went to greet Günther who had just entered the Diner.

"I have some good news for ya," said Günther as Emma poured him coffee. "I was talkin' to this retired gentleman at our church. He told me he used to live in Sterling and worked for the Journal Advocate running their presses. I asked him if he would be willing to work for us on a part-time basis. He said he would. I'm going to take him to the site tomorrow to take a look at the presses. He said he is pretty sure he can get them runnin'."

"Terrific! Now we can meet our December deadline. I've been telling all our advertisers to expect our first edition before Christmas," said Raimund.

"Me, too," said Günther. "Boy, the number jumping on board with us is greater than I expected. They all seem very excited."

"I'm making progress with the content. I'm working on an editorial article. I'm thinking also about including a poem."

"How about local news?" Günther asked.

"I went to the School Board meeting last week. They're going to meet again before Christmas. I'll put something together. They're talking about a bond initiative for a new elementary school. The community is really growing."

"The Chamber president said they'll have some growth news to report," said Günther.

"Also, Mayor Baker. We need to talk to him," said Raimund. "We'll have a religion section. So, I'll get in touch with St. Boniface and Zion Lutheran to give us a report."

"Have you established contact with the Associated Press?" Günther asked.

"Yes, we're going to have a hook-up with a teleprinter that we'll have to buy. Who knows what'll be on the national and international news come December. Whatever it might be, if it's important, we'll include it."

"You know, the Junior Guild has a Christmas Ball comin' up," said Günther. "I can cover it. I'll take my camera and get some pictures. It'll be a nice event to feature."

"We need to have a nice, big picture about Christmas on the front page," exclaimed Raimund. "Think about it, Günther, we've got time."

Günther took a gulp of coffee and said, "You know I'm hungry, I'm going to order some breakfast. Are you gonna order somethin'?"

"I can't, Günther. I've got to save my money. Can't afford to eat out."

Said Günther, "I'm living at home with my parents. They feed me and don't charge me rent. How about you? How are you keepin' groceries on your table?"

"I'm substitute teaching at the high school. They need me a lot. I'm making enough to make ends meet. My Mom calls and invites me home for dinner about once a week. At least I get one good meal. My cooking is not so good. Mom thinks I should live with them. I don't want to do that. I don't want them to have the extra burden of trying to take care of me."

Günther ordered bacon and eggs and hash browns. Raimund asked for a coffee refill.

# 31

# 𝕶𝖑𝖊𝖎𝖓 𝕶𝖔𝖚𝖗𝖎𝖊𝖗
Our First Edition
December 12, 1946

Editorial

# Family

At Christmas time we bring into the limelight the family of Jesus, and in our own lives Christmas is about our own families as well. It is a time when we show our love for each other with present giving and adhering to the familiar Christmas carol phrase: "I'll be home for Christmas." Last year, the Christmas of 1945 was a special one for my family – a family of ten siblings. It was the first time we all had been together since before "the war" had started. Over the years of the Great Depression and WWII, my family has struggled and has made many sacrifices. In addition to our assembly together, we had a lot to be thankful for. My brother Lukas survived a battle on a Pacific island where four thousand Americans died while annihilating eleven thousand Japanese. On the Pacific sea, brother Kristoff survived the sinking of an American aircraft carrier with eighteen hundred of his fellow sailors while more than four hundred died. Nineteen-forty-five had been a good year. The War had ended. Our president passed away, but the transition of power to our vice president went smoothly – a tribute to our democratic form of government. Economically, my family was doing well; my father had found plenty of work on farms and in town, and my mother was employed in the school cafeteria. My parents were optimistic about the upcoming year of 1946.

As a dozen of us assembled, my mother Lara, the fine cook that she is, supplied our traditional favorite foods. On Christmas Eve it was pinto bean soup and fresh baked buns with homemade butter. Cinnamon rolls and toasted fresh bread slices with butter were on the breakfast menu. For Christmas Day dinner, it was ham and gravy, mashed potatoes, green beans with bacon and onions, Waldorf salad, and banana-cream pie. On Christmas Day, we all attended Mass at St. Boniface. My mother played the organ while my sisters and I sang in the choir. Toward the end of the service, I sang the favored hymn, Ave Maria. I was reminded it was a young woman nearly two thousand years ago who by giving birth to Jesus, established the Holy Family, and made the Christmas celebration a reality. And now in the twentieth century, it was another woman, Lara, who made it possible for ten siblings to celebrate Christmas almost two thousand years later, and on Christmas of '45, we celebrated it together as the Knobloch Family.

## Christmas Tree

*German
Lutherans deserve the
recognition for establishing the
American Christmas tree tradition.*

*In mid-1800 America,
evergreen trees were arrayed
with candles, toys, gifts, and cakes home-made.*

*And wrapped all around was
dyed popcorn interlaced with berries on a string,
adding colorful beauty that these garlands bring.*

*By 1900 America had inaugurated
glass-blown ornaments and strings of electric light,
adorning trees brilliantly in the darkness of night.*

*Later to be added were
lengths of aluminum-coated, plastic strips,
simulating ice cycles hanging from tree branch tips.*

*In Colorado
the native Christmas trees of choice are spruce, fir or pine,
and any one of these could be seen in the decorated homes of Klein.*

By
Raimund
Knobloch

December 12, 1946

# The Associated Press

## Indian Prime Minister Jawaharlal Nehru Appeals to the United States and the Soviet Union to End Nuclear Testing and Start Disarmament

Prime Minister Nehru encourages the two superpowers to end nuclear testing and begin disarmament, stating, "Such an action would save humanity from the ultimate disaster." Nehru made these remarks while speaking to the Indian Parliament in New Delhi. Nehru further stated:

"A new weapon of unprecedented power, both in volume and intensity, with unascertained, and probably unascertainable, range of destructive potential in respect of time and space, that is both as regards duration and extent of its consequences, is being tested, unleashing its massive power, for use as a weapon of war. We are told that there is no effective protection against the hydrogen bomb and that millions of people may be exterminated by a single explosion. These are horrible prospects, and it affects us, nations, and people everywhere whether we are involved in wars or power blocs or not. Humankind has to awaken itself to the reality and face the situation with determination and assert itself to avert calamity."

From Nehru's point of view, disarmament in general and the elimination of nuclear weapons were integral to his doctrine of non-alignment with powerful nations.

# 32

# 𝕶𝖑𝖊𝖎𝖓 𝕶𝖔𝖚𝖗𝖎𝖊𝖗
August 15, 1947

## Heidi Klein and Herschel Wenzel Wed

Heidi Klein and Herschel Wenzel were married on Aug 5 at the Zion Lutheran Church in Klein, Colorado. Lutheran minister, the Rev. Helmut Schneider, officiated. Mrs. Wenzel, 24, is a buyer for Schuster's Department Store in Klein, working out of the Women's Fashions Department. She graduated from Wellesley College with a degree in economics. She is the daughter of Darlene J. Klein and Albert P. Klein. The bride's father is owner and president of the Board of Directors of the First National Bank of Klein and keeps a private law practice. The town of Klein derived its name from Albert Klein. The bride's mother is a stay-at-home parent. Mr. Wenzel, 25, is a partner with his father in the Wenzel Realty Co. in Klein. The groom graduated from Harvard University with a degree in architecture. He is the son of Harvey Wenzel, who lives with the groom's mother in Klein. The groom's mother, who is retired, was a Klein elementary school teacher. Mr. Wenzel's father is the president of Wenzel Realty.

The bride's and bridesmaid's gowns were designed and created by Vittorio of New York. The bride wore a white, long-sleeved gown and a cathedral-length veil. She carried a bouquet of pastel peonies, anemones, and buttercups, wrapped in a blush silk ribbon.

Zion Lutheran was filled with guests. Both sides of the main aisle were lined with ceramic bowls of pampa grass and terra cotta vessels of succulent cacti. The walkway of the main aisle was laced with white rose petals. A ceremonial arch of flowers and greenery was up front in the sanctuary with potted chrysanthemums and hydrangeas mounted on pedestals on each side. Ceramic vases of diverse colored roses sat on the window ledges. A garland of roses and fern fronds enveloped the railing of the long stairway to the pulpit. Mendelssohn's Wedding March was played by a stringed quartet (Gesine Baumgartner, viola; Sybille Koch, violin; Klaus Schwartz, violin; Lorenz Krause, cello). The new Mrs. Wenzel soloed with the violin, performing Vivaldi's Violin Concerto in A minor.

# 33

September 1947

9/1. We published the announcement of Heidi's wedding in The Kourier. I'm saddened by the thought she will now officially be severed from my life. I have fond memories of our past frequent encounters in high school. After all these years, I now know that I truly loved her. I wish her and Herschel nothing but the best.

9/2. The high school principal called me. Wanted to know if I could take over a class in sociology for the fall semester. The original teacher turned up pregnant, and the school policy is an expectant mother cannot teach. I consented. The added money earned will be a great help.

9/3. Günther has been hustling for advertisers. We have enough now where we think we can consider converting The Kourier from a monthly to a weekly. Will have to hire more help to run the presses. We have already hired a secretary. She is working out very well.

9/4. I'm working with a student intern from Colorado University. She is doing this for credit for her degree in journalism. Lives with her parents here in Klein, which is a good thing. We do not have the budget to pay her. Will work with her as a reporter.

9/5. Temperature in the seventies – a typical fall day. Did my clothes washing and drying in the coin-operated laundry.

9/6. Attended the ten o'clock Mass today. Sang in the choir. Went with Dad and Mom for brunch at Emma's. Dad paid. He is aware of my limited budget. Dad was painting a rental house for Mayor Baker. Mom said St. Boniface was growing. Getting a lot of young folks with kids. Will set up a nursery for the ten o'clock Mass. Prepared one week of lesson plans for my sociology class.

9/7. Walked to high school. Taught a sociology class at 10 am. Have 25 students.

9/8. Contacted seven business owners – discussed purchasing ads – was successful with three of them – one said she would think about it.

9/9. Cooked a pot of beans and baked bread – used Mom's recipes.

9/10. Worked on editorial for September edition. Began arranging page layouts.

9/11. Met with intern – reviewed article she had written. She did a good job. She has a lot of promise.

9/12. _____

9/13. Took inventory of supplies. Had to order more ink by phone. The supplier is in Chicago. Said they could get it to us by train in 4 days. Our publication deadline is on or before the 20th.

9/14. Had coffee with Mayor Baker at Emma's. He shared some statistics on the growth of the town with me. He and several members of the city council are recruiting businesses to come here. He's hoping that a Maytag franchisee will choose to come. Another possibility is an alfalfa pelletizing mill.

9/15. Went for a walk in the evening – took a walkway around Bubbling Pond.

# 34

A slight breeze swept over Bubbling Pond ruffling through Raimund's hair as he walked on a well-worn path along the eastern shore. Clad in a T-shirt and jeans, the low-temperate air cooled his bare arms and seemed to refresh his whole body. The ambience of twilight was in sharp contrast with the stuffiness of his office where he had spent the entire day. It was good to be outside, and he told himself that he needed the exercise. Winding his way around a Russian olive tree, he glanced over at the pond noting the small waves rippling the surface – creating a low lapping sound when they reached shore. He heard the chattering call of a killdeer, perhaps warning its mates of his pending approach. He watched the bird move quickly in the shallow water along the sandy shoreline searching for food. Moving on, the limbs of a tall mulberry tree shadowed the pathway – its dried summer fruits lay where he walked. He stopped under a giant cottonwood to see the frolicking movements of two squirrels, jumping from limb to limb, playing tag with one another. He wondered if it was a male and a female flirting with each other – reminding him of his school days.

As Raimund approached the dike on the south side of The Pond, the sky opened, and he could see all around him. To the west, he could see the small light of Venus just above the horizon, and a multitude of Milky Way stars began to appear above him. Above the tree line to the north, he saw the "KLEIN" letters on the water tower and the tall steeple of the Zion Lutheran Church. He advanced to the small array of cattails, sedges and reeds, found in the corner of the dike and the west shoreline; his sudden intrusion induced wary frogs to jump in the water, taking refuge. Reaching the north side, Raimund continued east on the pathway that lay between the long row of houses and The Pond. There in front of him, just thirty yards away, stood a three-story structure, surrounded by an eight-foot-high brick fence with a wood gate and a large letter "K" emblazoned on it. Raimund knew right away that this was the home of Albert Klein. Right next to it was a house amid construction. It had an original, peculiar design. Besides its large proportions, the single-story house was built of small limestone brick with a flat roof, overhangs and large upper windows. Raimund concluded that this was most likely the future home of Heidi and her architect husband, Herschel. He surmised that the volume of the house covered at least two large lots.

    Raimund continued his walk past back yards with barking dogs and playful children and parents sitting on porches marveling at the sunset. He arrived at his apartment refreshed. He relaxed on his couch listening to Mozart's Symphony No. 41 – a recording received from his dad on his twenty-fourth birthday. He removed a spiral notebook from an end-table desk drawer and began to write.

# 35

Raimund rose from his work desk abruptly, announcing to Günther working at his desk across the room, "Gotta go – its 11:30 and I'm scheduled to have lunch with Axel Eisenberger."

"Who's he?" Günther asked.

"He's the guy who's bringing the Western Auto Store to Klein. I'm going to interview him – he's from Pennsylvania. I'm told that he's from a German-Russian community – I want to see what he's got to say. I think a lot of our readers will be interested in him as well as Western Auto."

"Where ya goin' to eat?" Günther asked.

"Emma's," Raimund answered. "I'm paying for his lunch – I'll put it on our expense account. Will that be okay?"

"Sure thing – we can handle it. I think that store will do well here in Klein. A friend of mine told me he bought a set of tires from the one in Sidney – said he got a real good deal."

"I guess they're spreading all over the country – mostly in small towns – they must be doing something right," said Raimund.

Günther and Raimund were aware their readers were very interested in learning about the growth taking place in their community. They had already informed them of the apartment complexes that Herschel Wenzel was designing and building to accommodate the population expanse that was taking place. Wenzel was also designing a new style of ranch home, and his father had bought twenty-five acres of land from Albert Klein on which to build more than fifty houses. Instead of going to Sterling, local farmers were now buying their implements at John Deere and International Harvester businesses recently set up in Klein. Tom Baker bought the building next to his R&W and doubled the capacity of his grocery store; likewise, Klein Hardware added more space. The local Farmers Co-op built a cattle-auction facility on the edge of town next to the railroad tracks. Next to it, Denver Elevators began construction of two large storage cylinders – grain production in the area, stimulated by irrigation, had increased exponentially. It was rumored that a local was bringing a car dealership to Klein. Ford? Chevrolet? No one knew for sure.

The Town Council changed the diagonal car parking on Main Street to parallel parking to provide two extra traffic lanes for the increased volume of traffic moving through town. Patrons noticed several cars with Oklahoma license plates parked at Emma's Diner. The drivers were wearing long-sleeved shirts, newly pressed Wranglers, Stetsons, and boots. They told Emma they were negotiating oil leases with farmers – apparently, Phillips Petroleum believed there was oil beneath the prairie farms in the area.

## 36

# 𝕶𝖑𝖊𝖎𝖓 𝕶𝖔𝖚𝖗𝖎𝖊𝖗
### November 10, 1948

## Birth Announcement

Mr. and Mrs. Herschel Wenzel are happy to announce the birth of their daughter Monika Klein Wenzel on November 8, 1948, at the Logan County Hospital in Sterling. Monika was 6 pounds and 7 ounces at birth and was 18 inches long. The mother was formerly Miss Heidi Klein. This is the first grandchild of Albert and Darlene Klein and Harvey and Margit Wenzel.

---

"I see we published the birth of Heidi's kid," said Günther.

"Yes, that's some of the biggest news we've had here in Klein for a long time," said Raimund. "She comes from a fine pedigree. I'll bet she'll be a knockout when she grows up. I hope she has her mother's brains and ambition."

"Well, let's hope so," said Günther. "She probably won't get much gumption from her father. They say he's a lazy bastard – living on the money of his Dad. I hear, too, he's a gambler – plays a lot of poker with his drunken friends at Joe's Bar and takes a lotta trips to Vegas."

"He's a darned good architect," said Raimund. "Those apartments he's designed are pretty sleek, and his house is a real marvel."

"Have you been inside their house?" Günther asked.

"No, I haven't seen Heidi since right before she got married. Ran into her at Schuster's a couple of years ago."

"They say it is beautiful – exquisite crown molding and all that stuff," said Günther.

"With her elegant wardrobe and working in fashion at Schuster's, her home of downright elegance fits in right well," said Raimund. "I'm happy for her."

"Speaking of 'elegant living,' how is your apartment working out? You said once you wanted to move out," said Günther with a wry grin.

"I can't afford to move – rents have gone up. I'm just a couple of blocks from the school – I still have to substitute-teach, so my present location is really convenient."

"Well, let's hope we'll both get on the payroll real soon," said Günther. "It's been 'tough sleddin' for you these last couple of years. You've been workin' hard keepin' two jobs."

"You've been at the high school for a long time, what have you been teachin' lately?"

"Last week, I taught geometry – did it for four days. Before that it was history, and before that it was mechanical drawing. I've done it all. I'm learning more than the kids are."

# 37

Sitting at his office desk, Raimund picked up the receiver of his ringing phone. On the other end of the line was a familiar voice.

"Raimund, this is Katrin. Mom's in the hospital – we think she's had a stroke."

"When did that happen?"

"We think it started sometime this afternoon. When Kerstin and I got home from school, we found her lying on the kitchen floor. We called Dr. Shäfer – he came right away. As soon as he saw her, he had us help him put her in his car, and he drove her to Sterling – put her in the hospital."

"Why do they think it was a stroke?" Raimund asked.

"There's some paralysis on the left side of her face, and her conversation is confused. Dr. Shäfer says he didn't know what may have caused it. He sez it could be a blood clot or a hemorrhage."

"Does Hanna know about this?" Raimund asked.

"Yes, I called her, and she's with Mom now. She said she'll keep us informed. Dad knows about it – he's having a friend take him to see her tonight."

"I guess you and Kerstin can 'keep the home fires' burning, can't you?"

"Yes, we're cookin' supper now."

"Okay – thanks – let me know if you need anything."

Raimund hung up the phone in disbelief. He couldn't recall Lara at any time with ill health. She had never been sick. Lara had always been a supporter of his. Everything he did was for her. He knew she was proud of his accomplishments. The thought of losing her would take away his reason for living. He had no one else. She was his bedrock of existence. He wondered what she really thought about his newspaper endeavor. He was struggling. Was she disappointed? Now there was a possibility that Lara's time on earth had been shortened. He was now more determined to make The Kourier successful.

---

"Good mornin,' Tom. Good mornin,' Mr. Klein," said Emma. She set two cups of coffee in front of them and asked, "Whatcha gonna have?"

"I'll have the Denver omelet and two slices of toast," said Baker.

"Give me a bowl of oatmeal and one of your sweet rolls," said Klein. "I assume they're right out of the oven, aren't they?

"They sure are. So is our bread. It makes wonderful toast."

"Boy, it's cold out there," exclaimed Baker. "Sterling radio this morning said it was minus five at the airport."

"I bet it's colder than that here," said Klein. "There was so much ice on my thermometer, I couldn't read it this morning from my kitchen window.

"How are things going at Red and White? Are you using your new building now?"

"We sure are. It took us a while to hook up the new space to our old building. Finally got it done – started putting groceries in it two weeks ago. Customers really like it."

"Raimund Knobloch was in last week. Said he was going to send a reporter to come in and interview us and run a story on it in The Kourier. He said that things are pickin' up, and they're hirin' more staff."

"Well, they got a long way to go – they keep saying they're going to switch to a daily – I'll believe it when I see it."

"They must be makin' a little money – Raimund has kept up with his payments on our bank loan. I advertise all my specials every week. A lot of other businesses are advertisin' – they have a big account with Schuster's."

"I don't subscribe to it – wouldn't read it if I did. I get all my news from the Journal Advocate."

"Raimund said they were now havin' mail delivery in the rural areas," said Baker. "Subscriptions are increasin'."

"I heard that kid is still teaching," said Klein. "Things can't be all that good if he has to have a second job. I never thought that kid would amount to anything. You can't make any money teaching. My guess is that is what he'll end up doing."

The conversation lagged as Emma arrived with their breakfast and renewed their coffee.

"I think you're shortchangin' that young man," Baker said. "He's payin' his bills. Has a lot of smarts, and he works hard. Give him time. Time will tell."

# 38

# 𝕶𝖑𝖊𝖎𝖓 𝕶𝖔𝖚𝖗𝖎𝖊𝖗

Friday March 12, 1950

## WE ARE GOING DAILY

We are pleased to announce that your Klein Kourier hereon will be published daily as a morning edition. Thanks for your support. We are proud to serve the Klein community, and we are looking forward to being an integral part of Klein for many years to come.

---

The Kourier staff had worked frantically all day Thursday to get Friday's edition ready. The turnaround each day with new stories and new copies was challenging and physically exhausting. It was 11:30 p.m. when Raimund relaxed on his sofa in his apartment and took out his diary to mark the important day of The Kourier being printed as a daily. In Raimund's mind, this was a monumental success. This was the true indicator that he and Günther had achieved their goal. They had truly established a newspaper – aptly named the Klein Kourier.

# March 1950

3/12. Published The Kourier as a daily newspaper today. This has been our goal all along. We have succeeded. We have <u>truly</u> established a newspaper. It is a significant event in the eyes of the world and in our eyes as well. Although she won't say it to me, I know my Mom is proud of my accomplishment.

3/13. I perused my Bible reference volume searching for passages on giving thanks. It pointed me to the Old Testament: Daniel 2:23. "I thank and praise you, God of my ancestors: You have given me wisdom and power."

3/14. Mom is making progress in her recovery. The paralysis on the side of her face had disappeared. Dr. has her on a blood thinner to prevent a clot from reappearing. She had sustained a slight paralysis on her right side. Her weekly physical therapy has helped her to regain all of her normal physical movement. My dad has been a great help with her recovery.

3/15. Have been invited to give a talk on creative writing to the high school English class. I told them if they want to be writers, they should do it every day. Keeping a diary is a good way to start.

3/16. Taught world history for three days to junior-level students. Found out how little I know. Good class!

3/17. Have had cold weather for a week. The snow has finally disappeared. Looking forward to spring.

3/18. I took Diane Mosely to the Winterfest Ball, sponsored by the Rotary Club. Diane is a choir mate of mine at St. Boniface. Had a really good time. We had to walk in the cold. Hope to ask her out again.

3/19. I had Mom write down her recipe for making banana-cream pie. I tried it last weekend. Turned out pretty well – even the meringue was good. Baker's Red and White had a sale on bananas to which I took advantage.

3/20. We are nearing the point where Günther and I can take a salary. Will start saving to buy a car – also, to upgrade my living facilities.

3/21. The twins will be graduating from Colorado University this spring. Konrad with a degree in geology, and Kurt in business administration. It is hard to believe they are already finishing college. I hardly know them. they are mature young men. Steffi will soon graduate from high school. She likes Colorado A&M – they have a teacher education program in which she is interested.

3/22. Günther announced his engagement to a girl he met at CSCE. Looking forward to meeting her.

# 39

Harvey Wenzel drove his Cadillac with Wenzel Realty displayed on each front door in front of a newly constructed home and parked. Raimund emerged from the front seat saying, "I like this cul de sac spot, Mr. Wenzel. Have a little more privacy and less traffic."

"This has three bedrooms. That's what you want, isn't it?"

"Yes sir, I want one for guests and one for my office. I do a lot of work at home."

"This one has all Maytag appliances," said Wenzel. "We've worked out a deal with the Maytag dealer here in Klein. He honors a maintenance contract to the buyer for two years."

"I like the looks of it. And the flat roof! You don't see many of those around," exclaimed Raimund.

"My son designed this one to fit neatly into the trapezoidal lot. You aren't going to see any other like it out here," said Wenzel.

"Herschel sure does good work. His houses really stand out," said Raimund.

"Thanks – I spent a hell of a lot of money at Harvard gettin' him educated. Finally gettin' some return on my investment."

Wenzel opened the locked front door leading to an entryway with an oak wood floor. Looking into the living and dining rooms, Raimund noted doors, cabinets, and woodwork also constructed of oak. He liked the "natural wood" look. The cushioned carpet throughout the house supported a comfort to his walk; it was a luxurious experience he had not had. He acknowledged to himself a real appreciation for the laundry room; coin-operated laundry would be a thing of the past. The view of the prairie from the screened-in porch was very appealing to him. The back yard was covered with Kentucky bluegrass, and two small silver-leafed poplars had been planted thirty yards from the house. Living in a new house – his own – was an exciting thought. He took solace in knowing his hard work had finally paid off. He was fortunate. He quickly said a prayer of thanks.

"I'm very interested in buying this," Raimund said as they walked to the car.

"We can help with the financin.' We have an arrangement with First National in gettin' loans."

"Thanks, Mr. Wenzel. I think I'll have to go elsewhere. Mr. Klein has never been a supporter of the Knobloch family. He turned both my father and me down when we applied at First National. I've worked with a bank in Sterling for all my business dealings. They said they would work with me."

"Klein handles all my legal work. So, we'll have to deal with him sometime down the road," said Wenzel. "However, he has no 'skin-in-the-game' on this. He should be a 'pussy cat'."

Driving back to Wenzel's office, Raimund asked, "Are you and Mrs. Wenzel enjoying your granddaughter?"

"Boy, are we!" exclaimed Wenzel. "That little cuss is smart as hell. Heidi's teachin' her to play the piano. We all read to her. She picks things up quickly. She just had her third birthday. The missus takes care of her while Heidi's at work."

"How's Heidi doin'?" She's still at Schuster's, isn't she?"

"Yes, she really likes it. Has found her calling. Dresses like a movie star. Her father still takes pretty good care of her. Her work in fashion is a far cry from her economics education. She's a smart lady. Has a good understanding of women's clothing design. Picked it up quickly. I've gotta hand it to her."

"Give her my best, Mr. Wenzel. Tell her I said hello."

# 40

Signing the final papers for Raimund to buy his home took place in the meeting room of Wenzel Realty. Wendel Winston, legal attorney for Logan County Bank of Sterling and Raimund sat across the table from Wenzel and Klein. Klein, with a scowl, slumped in his chair away from the table, displayed body language that showed he would rather be somewhere else. He gave no acknowledgement to Raimund's presence; he ignored him as well all the others in the room. Following brief introductions to Winston, Wenzel began discussion of the contract. He invited Winston to explain the narrative leading to the transfer of funds to Wenzel Realty and the monthly payment obligation of Raimund and the interest on the principal he would be charged. He then asked Klein if he had any recommended changes to the documents. Klein said nothing and simply moved his head from side to side; he had no changes. The session concluded with all parties asked to sign at specific locations on the paperwork.

With the final signature, Klein finally spoke, "Mr. Knobloch, I hope you have paid off all your other notes before taking this one on."

Raimund, not expecting the comment, hesitated a moment, pausing to control his anger before responding, "Mr. Klein, my debts should really be no concern of yours, but since you brought it up, the answer is a resounding yes. Furthermore, I did it without any help or support from you. You, with the most resources of anyone in the community, could have been the one to help me. **But you did not!** Supporting a community newspaper should have been an obligation you should have willingly accepted. **But you did not!** Thank God, other members of the community believed in us, even though **you did not**.

Klein said nothing more as he cowered with a lowered head and stuffed his papers in his leather briefcase. Acknowledging no one, he abruptly left the room.

# 41

As the morning sun shone on Bubbling Pond, a lone boat floated on the midst of its surface, wobbling as tiny waves struck its side. How it got there could not be at once ascertained – if it were an oarsman, he or she was not visible. Was it a boat unknowingly broken from its tether to the boathouse dock that moved out to the deep water?

That same morning, Heidi awakened at 3 a.m. and realized that her husband Herschel was not at her side. Last night he told her he was going to play cards at Joe's Bar, and he would be home at midnight. "But where was he?" Heidi asked herself. He still wouldn't be at Joe's – it closed at midnight. Had he been kidnapped? Had he been murdered? Did he have an accident? Heidi called her father. Albert Klein advised, "Go back to bed; most likely he's hanging out at the home of one of his friends, and the time is gotten away from them. He'll turn up."

At 6 a.m., Herschel still had not come home. Heidi was now very anxious and worried. She called Harvey Wenzel. After hearing her story, Wenzel went to the Klein police. They began a search in the neighborhood near the bar, his home and around the town. They discovered his Jaguar parked near Bubbling Pond. Bystanders, drawn to the scene by the presence of police, pointed them to the unmanned boat out on the pond. Several police climbed into boats and paddled out to the boat, hoping to find Herschel. Seeing no evidence of him, they invited divers from Sterling to conduct a search. They found him at dusk, submerged in six feet of water, not far from the shore. Tied to his legs were two concrete blocks.

Two days later, Herschel's obituary (written by Heidi) was published in The Kourier. The cause of death was not mentioned. Speculation by some was that he had been murdered. Most others thought it was suicide. It was rumored that he had huge gambling debts with locals and had lost money in Las Vegas. Rumors floated around about his large losses in the stock market. Some said he had invested in a uranium mine near Grand Junction that went belly-up. Still, others gossiped his marriage was not going well, and Heidi had threatened to leave him.

His funeral, held at Zion Lutheran, was attended by many. Folding chairs were set up in the vestibule and inside the main aisle to accommodate the large crowd. Günther and Raimund found a seat in the choir loft. They saw Heidi – a black veil lay over her head and covered her face. Monika was at her side and her parents and the Wenzels were sitting next to them. The casket, just inside the sanctuary, was flanked with two lighted candles. Baskets of flowers from well-wishers filled the whole front of the church, supplying a brightened beauty that contradicted the sadness of the occasion.

From the heightened pulpit, the Rev. Helmut Schneider eulogized Herschel, citing his many accomplishments and his laudable, personal attributes.

Schneider said, 'Sometimes things happen that we don't understand, and perhaps we'll never know why they occurred. But that is God's plan. He reveals to us what need to know and when we need to know it. Today we pray for understanding. We pray for understanding the will of God."

The Rev. Schneider then added, "In **Chapter sixteen, verse thirteen, John writes**: When the Spirit of truth comes, he will guide you into all the truth, for he will not speak on his own authority, but whatever he hears he will speak, and he will declare to you the things that are to come."

A large entourage of cars followed the hearse carrying Hershel's body to his final resting place, the Klein Memorial Cemetery, on the edge of town. Günther parked his car about a hundred yards from the gravesite, and he and Raimund hurriedly walked, arriving just in time to see the Rev. Schneider presenting a crucified Christ icon to Heidi. She held it tightly to her breast, stoically accepting his blessing as he placed both hands on her head. She handed it to Monika to scrutinize. With eyes closed, Heidi sat motionless, listening to the pastor's last call to welcome Herschel Wenzel into God's Kingdom.

When the final words and prayers were said, mourners began to walk toward their cars. Some stopped to visit with Heidi, offering condolences and expressing their sorrow. Raimund stood in line, taking his turn to offer sympathy. He reached out to clasp Heidi's hand as he stepped in front of her. He wanted to say something, but he couldn't – the words would not come out. His eyes moistened as he looked into her eyes. He squeezed her hand and then wrapped his arms around her. He held her tightly for a few seconds. She put her arms around him and began to cry. Releasing his grasp, he stepped back, and turned away – he still could not speak.

Walking back to the car, Raimund said nothing to Günther – he had no words. His thoughts focused on Heidi and the pain she was experiencing. He imagined her grief and sadness to be overwhelming. A fortunate woman with great wealth and a beautiful family, now facing a sudden "bend in the road" she was not expecting. Heidi is a wonderful person. She did not deserve this. But God's view on the world is not to protect only the righteous; the Lord has said that if you follow Him, there will be suffering. Raimond stepped into the car with moistened eyes. He stayed silent as they rode home.

# 42

Tom Baker said to his assistant who had just arrived for work, "I'm meeting with a couple of guys over at Emma's."

"Okay, remember we got that load of vegetables comin' in at ten. You'll need to be here to sign off on it," said Max Boxberger, the R&W manager.

"I should be back by then."

Stepping through the diner front door, Tom saw Günther and Raimund, sitting at a small table in the back and waving to him.

"Have you ordered yet?" he asked.

"No, we were waiting for you," said Günther.

Emma came up to them, asking for their orders. She poured a cup of coffee for Tom – refilling the cups of the other two.

Raimund picked up the conversation, "Tom, we know you bought the old Schuster building when they moved to another location, and we were wondering if you would like to sell it."

"I think I would if the price is right. Whatcha gonna do with it?"

"We wanna move the newspaper operation there. The presses, the staff, the "whole enchilada," said Günther.

"Do you think it's big enough?" Tom asked.

"We think so. You know it's two-story, and it's got a basement and all those offices upstairs. We think it'll work well," said Raimund.

"How you gonna pay for it? Get a loan?" Tom asked.

"Yes sir," said Günther. "We were wonderin' if you might help us out with gettin' the financin'."

"How's your balance sheet workin' out these days? Are ya' in the black?"

"Yes sir, said Günther. "We've been aggressive in goin' for the advertisin'."

"And our readership has increased," Raimund interjected.

"I could rent the building to ya'."

"We'd rather buy," said Günther. "We've talked and thought about this for a long time. We think the best thing for this next step is to have our own facility."

"What are ya' askin' for your building?" Günther asked.

"50 grand," Tom answered.

"It'll probably take another twenty-five to move and renovate," Günther added. "We are meeting with our accountant next week. We're having him help us with our business plan. He'll help us figure out what our worth is."

"If we borrow money, would you recommend we present our case to Logan County Bank in Sterling?" Raimund asked.

"Yes, and I can help you with that."

"We have a lot of options to consider. We'll let you know what we decide after our accountant meeting," said Raimund.

"Thanks for your time and friendship. You have been a great help to us over the years. We owe a lot of our success to you, Tom. You are a valuable member of the Klein community."

# 43

Fritz Werner entered the new Kourier building and asked the receptionist, "Is Raimund in? My name is Fritz Werner – I am one of his former teachers at the high school. I'd like to speak with him for a few minutes if he is available."

"Have a seat and let me call him." After a short conversation, she said, "He'll see you – go right in."

"Good afternoon, Raimund," exclaimed Werner, extending his hand.

"Good afternoon to you, Mr. Werner. My gosh, I haven't seen you since I graduated. So nice to see you. Have a seat."

"How long have you been in this building?" Werner asked.

"Two weeks – we're still moving stuff in," Raimund replied.

"It's a very nice facility. That neon sign out there is impressive," exclaimed Werner.

"Thank you, Mr. Werner. What brings you in here?"

"Several of us musicians in the town have been talkin' about starting a community symphony orchestra. We'd like to have a meeting and invite people to come and see if there is enough interest in it. We wanted to advertise it in The Kourier. Whatta ya' think?"

"I think it's a splendid idea," Raimund answered. "There's a lot of musical talent in this town. I bet there's a lot of folks who'd take part. I know I would. I'd like to 'dust-off' my clarinet and give it a try. I bet Heidi Wenzel would play. I hear she's always putting quartets together and playing in her church. If you can get her, she'll bring in a lot of people with her."

"We'd like to start a support group – a 'friends of the symphony' society to help with the concerts and with the fundraising," added Werner.

"Where are you going to have the concerts? In the high school auditorium?" Raimund asked.

"Yes, my principal said he'd go to the school board to get the okay."

"Let me know when you're ready, and we'll put the ad in the paper free of charge, and I'll write an editorial supporting it."

———————

It seemed to Raimund that it was just a short time ago he was playing his clarinet in the high school orchestra. He had practiced a couple of times before now, but he knew he still had a long way to go to overcome his "rustiness." Fritz Werner had assembled 31 musicians for the first symphony practice in the high school orchestra room. Despite the volunteer nature of the orchestra, Werner had previously conducted individual "auditions" to assess the competence of each musician. He already had determined Heidi would be the first chair, and she was sitting close to the conductor's podium. As in his high school days, Raimund sat in the clarinet section – about thirty feet from the conductor.

Werner had them play the traditional French piece, Burgundian Carol, by Bernard de la Monnoye. He stopped and started the group, explaining and critiquing, suggesting ways to improve. After an hour of intense playing, he brought things to a halt and announced a fifteen-minute break. Raimund and Heidi approached the water fountain at the same time.

"Good evening, Heidi. How are you?"

"Very well, Raimund, thank you."

Raimund waited for her to take in a swallow of water and wipe her lips before he asked, "How are things going at Schuster's?"

"Great. Our new facility is working out well. We're getting a lot of new clientele. I'm sure our advertising in The Kourier has something to do with it."

"Thanks, it is comforting to be validated with your testimony."

"Looks like the newspaper is going well," said Heidi.

"It is. We have 15 employees and a couple of interns. We're all working hard now that we are 'a daily.' I'd like to visit more with you. How about meeting for ice cream at the drugstore when we finish here?"

"I'd like that. I can't stay too long. I must pick up Monika – she's at my mother's house."

# 44

The town siren had sounded five minutes prior, the sure sign of a pending danger. The weatherman on Sterling's KCDO TV was trying his best to give the latest information on the storm's location and its expected path. Likewise, a KPMX Radio announcer was alerting listeners to take shelter in basements, bathrooms, and closets.

Raimund hung up his office phone. He had just talked to Lara and Walter about the tornado that was heading toward Klein. The two of them, now empty nesters, were taking refuge in their cellar. He rushed out of his office and yelled to all the staff in the large workroom, "Hey you all! Get to the basement! A tornado is coming this way! Should be here in any minute! Quick, get down in the basement."

The wind blew over Bubbling Pond at eighty miles an hour producing waves three feet high, untethering boats, and throwing them offshore onto bare ground. Planks from the dock, ripped loose by the pounding water, were uplifted by the fast-moving air and scattered. A strong gust struck the concession stand with such a force, it exploded into small pieces, broadcasting debris over nearby streets, yards, and roofs. Picnic tables and benches disintegrated into splintered fragments. Several cottonwoods, unable to resist the blast, tilted, uprooted, and fell into the water.

Among the presses with his staff, Raimund heard a continuous rumble, something like a nearby train. It reminded him of an open car window while driving 60 miles an hour. He looked out the basement window – sheets of tin were bumping up and down and whizzing by on the street. He heard a sudden crash of glass – splinters fell to the floor, accompanied by large, baseball-sized hail stones. Some of the staff screamed with fright. One yelled out, "What the hell's goin' on?"

Raimund yelled back, "Hang on – you're in the safest place you can be – it'll be over in just a few minutes. Stay with us!"

---

# 𝕶𝖑𝖊𝖎𝖓 𝕶𝖔𝖚𝖗𝖎𝖊𝖗

May 6, 1953

## Tornado Strikes Klein

A powerful storm swept northeastward across Logan County in the afternoon of May 5, 1953. It carved a path of destruction, nearly 40 miles in length. The continuous path of damage was over 20 miles across the heart of Logan County. The tornado, up to one-mile wide at times, initially touched down northeast of Fleming and finally lifted 6 miles east of Klein. An assessment in the aftermath revealed extensive areas of damage, including farm buildings west of Klein, and businesses and homes in eastern Klein. Farmers reported extensive damage to crops and irrigation equipment.

So far only one fatality has been reported. Other reports of injuries ranging from broken bones to minor cuts and lacerations to more than fifty people have been filed. Trucks were flipped along the highway east of Klein, and power poles were snapped or blown down. Several hundred homes were left without electricity. The tornado overturned 9 railroad cars and destroyed a lumber car on the Burlington and Missouri Railway. It also flattened the quonset gymnasium of the high school and destroyed the two-story, wood structure of Denver Elevators. The tin roof of The Kourier building was blown off, and the top floor received severe water damage. In addition to the ravaging winds, the accompanying thunderstorm produced damaging hail up to the size of baseballs. Preliminary estimates provided by town officials show nearly 100 homes damaged and another 50 destroyed.

# 45

The tranquil surface of Bubbling Pond reflected the rays of the hot July sun as Klein residents congregated on its sandy shore. Some brought chairs – others brought blankets. Some carried basket lunches – others held on to large, collapsed umbrellas. They surveyed all around as they walked, deciding where best to find their entourage. A six-member band was playing from a temporary platform stage, placed near the water. Bubbling Pond was in the background as attendees watched and listened to the patriotic music the band was playing for the occasion. It was July Fourth, and Klein was holding its annual celebration of the nation's independence.

At the newly constructed concession stand, Raimund stood in line, waiting to order Nehi sodas for Heidi, Monika and himself. Sodas in hand, he walked back to the table where Heidi and Monika were sitting. Heidi had arranged to have a concession table reserved close to the bandstand. He set the bottles down amongst the food and utensils Heidi had spread on the table. A plate of egg-salad sandwiches, a bowl of potato salad, deviled eggs, chips, celery and carrot sticks, blueberry muffins, and place settings for three were neatly displayed.

"It's right nice of you, Heidi, to provide this food for us," said Raimund as he sat down.

"My pleasure. My housekeeper prepared it. She usually prepares the evening meal for us when I'm working. Thank you for inviting me. I haven't been to this celebration for many years. Herschel and I used to come every year. Ever since he passed, I had not wanted to visit Bubbling Pond. The Pond brought back too many depressing memories. At first, I was reluctant to come today, but since <u>you</u> were the one who asked me, I convinced myself I ought to be here."

"I'm glad you came," said Raimund.

"I am, too," said Heidi.

"How about you, Monika? Raimund asked. "Are you happy to be here?"

"Yes I am. I like music. My mother is teaching me to play the piano."

"You like music, don't you, Mr. Knobloch? My mother told me you play in the orchestra with her."

"Yes, I like music. Your mother and I used to play in our high school orchestra many years ago. Our teacher took us to a concert in Sterling where they played a composition by a famous musician named Wolfgang Amadeus Mozart. Have you ever heard his music?"

"No, no I haven't."

"You will someday," said Raimund. "Someday you'll hear his music, and when you do, you'll never forget it. In my mind, Mozart has written some of the best music the world has ever heard. He's written over forty compositions. I have recordings of most of them."

Raimund turned to Heidi, "Do you remember the Mozart concert we went to in high school?"

"Yes, I remember it well."

"Do you remember that on the way home on the bus we never stopped talking about it? We both were astounded by how beautiful Mozart's Clarinet Concerto was. It 'blew us out of the water'."

"Yes, listening to the clarinet soloist accompanied by all those strings was a fantastic experience. It must have lasted over half an hour. We were enthralled. I've never forgotten that evening."

The threesome munched on the food as the band played. The music stopped for all to hear Mayor Baker's words over a loudspeaker. The mayor spoke of the freedoms citizens have in the USA for which they should be grateful. He called for a "moment of silence" to remember the Klein servicemen who gave their lives in the "two wars." His last remark was:

"Please plan to stay or come back this evening to observe the spectacular fireworks display over Bubbling Pond."

# 46

*February* 1956

2/1. Received three inches of snow today. Expecting below-freezing temperatures tonight and tomorrow.

2/2. Traded-in my car to buy a used 1952 Bel Air Chevrolet for $550. Bought it at the local Chevrolet dealer. They threw in new floor mats. Gave me $100 for my old Ford.

2/3. Went to orchestra practice tonight. Preparing for our upcoming concert in May. Afterwards, Heidi and I went to Emma's for coffee and pie.

2/4. Worked on my editorial for the next-day-after next edition. Supporting a school bond issue for a new gymnasium for the high school.

2/5. Günther supplied an update on our finances. Supply costs have increased 5% over the last twelve months. Discussed potential raises versus bonuses for employees.

2/6. Took Heidi to see *The Ten Commandments* at the Fox Theater in Sterling last night. Featured many Hollywood stars. We both liked it. Didn't get home until 12:30.

2/7. Went to church at 10 am. Took Mom in a wheelchair. Sang in the choir. Mom is no longer playing the organ. She had been doing it for almost thirty years. Had the usual breakfast at Emma's with Mom and Dad. Dad's physical strength is waning. This time I paid.

2/8. Had lunch with Heidi in Schuster's Dining Room. She was exquisitely dressed. I had lobster bisque. Heidi had a lettuce salad. We shared a slice of apple pie.

2/9. Called Hanna to wish her a Happy Birthday.

2/10. Heidi invited me to her home after orchestra practice for coffee and cake. Listened to a recording of Bach's Prelude No. 1. She asked me to sing the Ave Maria as it played. I consented. She invited Monika to come and listen.

2/11. It snowed again. Got five inches.

2/12. Today is Abraham Lincoln's birthday. Picked up an article on him from the Associated Press that we published in The Kourier. Lincoln was an honorable and accomplished man.

2/13. Attended Chamber of Commerce luncheon meeting. The speaker was Senator Calvin Walden from Sterling. Spoke on the state's economic growth as a center of electronic and high-technology manufacturing.

2/14. Valentine's Day: Had a dozen red roses delivered to Heidi's office.

# 47

Presiding over the Klein City Council Meeting, Mayor Tom Baker read out loud the following memorandum:

TO: Whom It May Concern

FROM: Albert Klein  *Albert Klein*

DATE: March 1, 1958

SUBJECT: Price Increase in Klein Water Allocation

    Let it be known that the current price of water distributed to the city of Klein ($5,200/acre-feet) will be increased by 40% to a new price of $7,280/acre-feet, effective January 1, 1957. This increase is dictated by: (1) The higher cost of water received from the South Platte River Authority; (2) The larger volume of water needed by the city; (3) The need for dredging ditch connecting South Platte River to Bubbling Pond; (4) Bubbling Pond dike upgrade; and (5) Higher wages for ditch rider.

---

    "Thanks for meetin' with me," said Mayor Baker as he sat down at a side table in Emma's Diner where Raimund was sitting.

    "You bet, Tom, what's going on?"

    "You've probably heard by now – Klein wants to increase what he charges for water by 40%."

"Yes, I talked to Councilman Magnuson the other day. He was pretty upset about it."

"We've done the calculation, and that means each household will have to pay an added $83 per year. That's way too much for 'em. They're already payin' more than $200 a year."

"I'm paying about $24 a month. With my new house and new lawn, I'm using a lot more water," said Raimund.

"I talked to Albert. He claims he has a lot of infrastructure issues he must take care of. Sez his ditch is silting up and the Bubbling Pond dike is crumbling. Sez he has to pay more now for South Platte water."

"What did you tell him?"

"I told him that I understood what his concerns were, but I did not believe the citizens of Klein should pay for his infrastructure costs. I said those were investment costs that he should pay for, not us. I said we should pay for the increased costs of water he delivers and a minimal ditch transport cost, but that is all."

"What would that cost the citizens?" asked Raimund.

"Our financial guy on the council calculates it to be 12 percent which is about 25 bucks a year. Three fourths of that is for the water cost increase and the other fourth is for transport."

"What did Klein say to that?"

"He was hoppin' mad. Said it was way too low. He argued that he had not raised the rate for five years. Said he always had absorbed the increases over the years. He wasn't going to budge from his proposal."

"What do you want me to do?" asked Raimund.

"I want you to write an editorial, telling the folks how he's trying to fleece us. We can give you all the numbers to substantiate our position. Also, we want to announce that we're hiring a water-rights lawyer outta Sterling to negotiate with Klein. The folks need to know what's goin' on."

"I'll do what I can, but you know how Klein feels about me. You know he has never been a fan of mine. He's never appreciated the Knoblochs, particularly me."

"Well, if he doesn't listen to you, we'll take the son-of-a-bitch to court. Our residents have already been beaten to death with rising prices. Enough is enough. It's time for Albert Klein to share more of the burden."

Emma poured them more coffee and took their order.

# 𝕶𝖑𝖊𝖎𝖓 𝕶𝖔𝖚𝖗𝖎𝖊𝖗

April 8, 1959

## Obituary

Walter Axel Knobloch

Walter Axel Knobloch passed away on April 6, 1959, in his sleep at his home in Klein. Walter was born in Toronto, Ontario, Canada, on March 9, 1895. He served his country in World War I in the Canadian Army as an infantryman, enlisting and rising to the level of sergeant. He came to the US where he met Lara Dieffenbach from St. Petersburgh, Colorado who became his wife in 1920. He was designated a US citizen in 1931. Walter was a laborer on farms near Fleming and Klein. He also earned his living as a carpenter and painter. Walter was a member of St. Boniface Catholic Church and was instrumental in physically obtaining the present-day church building. Walter was preceded in death by his parents (Gerwin and Lena Knobloch), a sister (Gerda Knobloch Richter) and a brother (Ernst Knobloch), all from Toronto. He is survived by his wife, Lara, and ten children: Lukas, Kristoff, Raimund, Hanna, Kurt, Konrad, Stefan, Steffi, Kerstin, and Katrin. His funeral service will be on Thursday, April 10 at 10 a.m. at St. Boniface Catholic Church. Interment will follow at Klein Memorial Cemetery.

"We've got all your stuff in boxes in the living room," said Raimund as he helped Lara up the steps to the front door of his house. "Had your bedroom furniture brought in yesterday."

Raimund invited Lara to live with him. She was reluctant to leave her home she had occupied with her family for nearly thirty years. But Raimund did not want her living alone. He was now the primary caregiver. All his other siblings had left Klein. Furthermore, he had a housekeeper, Olga Tanneberger, who could help with meeting Lara's needs.

Once in the bedroom, Raimund asked, "Do you like the color? You said you wanted it to be mauve?"

"Yes, I like it very much. It is most soothing. It will go very well with my light-blue bed spread."

"How about the bed? Is that where you want it? Or should we put it against the other wall?

"It's okay. But I want the dresser over here," she said, pointing to the location. Raimund proceeded to move it to her specified site.

"Figure out where you want your pictures, and this weekend I'll hang them for you," said Raimund.

He opened the sliding glass door and walked out onto the porch, with Lara following close behind.

"I think I'm goin' to like it out here," said Lara.

"It's a great place to read a good book – you can pull that shade down over there to keep the sun out," said Raimund.

In the kitchen, he showed her an empty cupboard where she could put her pots and pans. "This weekend, I'll take you to Red & White so you can get the groceries you want. Also, we can stop by Western Auto and buy you a TV for your bedroom."

"Boy, you're goin' to downright spoil me, son," said Lara as she sat down in a soft chair across from the sofa where Raimund was sitting.

"That's what we want to do, Mom. You deserve it. Olga will be here at eleven – she will help you arrange your bedroom and prepare some lunch for you. I'm heading back to work and should be home around six. I'm taking you out to dinner – Emma always has a special entrée on Thursday nights – it should be good."

# 49

"Okay folks, that's enough – you're soundin' good – we are just about there," said Fritz Werner, conductor of the Klein Symphony Orchestra. "Let's take a break. Be back here in fifteen minutes." The orchestra had been rehearsing for the upcoming concert, just two weeks away.

When Heidi stood and turned around to face the members, Raimund quickly referenced in his mind just how beautiful she was. She was dressed in a matching azure-blue headscarf and blouse, bright gold-colored pants, and sandals. Her long, waved hair flowed backward through the scarf, and her pant-legs halted right below the calf. The bareness of her arms, ankles and feet displayed a beautiful brown tan from the sun. Her fingernails and toenails were painted a brilliant red, complementing her reddened, alluring lips. She approached Raimund just as he was about to exit the room.

"Would you like to come to my house tonight?" she asked. "My housekeeper just baked a cherry pie, and a slice of it along with a cup of coffee sounds pretty good."

"Yes, I can. I'd like that."

"Do you think you can stop by your house and pick up your Mozart Clarinet Concerto recording? I'm in the mood for listening to it."

"Yes, I can do that. No trouble at all," said Raimund eagerly.

It was a little after nine o'clock when Heidi answered the door to let Raimund into her home. She led him through the living room to a large sitting room where a phonograph was already playing a Bach symphony.

"Would you like some coffee?

"Absolutely, with both sugar and cream, please."

"Do you want ice cream with your pie?"

"Absolutely – two scoops if I may."

"Is Monika here?" he asked.

"No, she's staying with her grandmother Wentzel. The two of them are very close. Margit sez Monika reminds her of Herschel."

"How old is Monika?"

"She's sixteen. Won't be long and she'll be off to college."

They conversed excitedly as they ate – Raimund relaying stories about The Kourier and Heidi describing experiences at Schuster's. Heidi collected the plates and forks and replenished their coffee cups.

"Let's listen to Mozart. Go ahead and put him on," she commanded.

They listened intently, sipping coffee, saying nothing as the music surged from the maple-encased Philco. On the two-seat sofa, Heidi sat next to Raimund, her hand overlapping the top of his. They were silent until the phonograph went mute.

"That is beautiful stuff," exclaimed Raimund. "Every time I hear that clarinet play, it reminds me of our high school days and you. It was attending that Mozart concert when I really got to know you. I developed feelings for you that have not gone away. All these years, I've never forgotten you. Today my passions are just as strong as they were then."

"Well, in the last couple of years, I must admit that those same feelings I had for you have been rekindled. There is no doubt that they were forced into dormancy because of my father, but getting back with you has brought some needed excitement to my life. I've enjoyed every recent minute I've spent with you. Thanks for being a part of my life when I so desperately needed understanding and love."

Heidi arose from her seat and asked, "Would you like some more coffee?"

"No thanks, I'm wired now higher than a kite."

"What do you call that second movement of Mozart's concerto? Is it the Adagio?" Heidi asked.

"Yes, it is. Why do you ask?"

"It is slower than the first, and I'm wondering if we could dance to it. Would you like to try it?"

"I'd love to," said Raimund. "Let's go for it."

"See if you can place the needle where it starts," enjoined Heidi.

Raimund placed his arm around Heidi's tiny waist as the music began. He pulled her close and clasped her right hand tightly. Heidi placed her head on his chest and reached her left hand to the back of his neck. Raimund was captivated by the fragrance from Heidi's hair and the swaying movement of her hips next to his. They moved slowly in two-step circles around the small room, keeping time with the beguiling Mozart sounds. Heidi raised her head and softly kissed Raimund's lips. She looked into his eyes and said, "Thanks for coming tonight."

"Thank you!" shouted Raimund. "I've been wanting to do this for a long time. I had given up. I never thought it would happen."

# 50

"Would you like to go to the Christmas Ball?" Raimund asked Heidi as they dug their spoons into the sundaes they had ordered. The orchestra rehearsal had finished thirty minutes earlier and now they were seated in a booth at Bass's Drug.

"Yes, I would. When is it?"

"Two weeks from tomorrow – it's Friday, December 18$^{th}$. Are you free that night?"

"Yes I am. But I can't stay out too late. The next day I have to drive to Boulder and pick up Monika. She'll be out of school for her Christmas break."

"How's she doin?" Raimund asked.

"I talked to her two days ago. She said she had all 'As' going into finals. Sez she still likes architecture, so she's going to stay in it at least for the next semester. Herschel really encouraged her to go into it. They were very close – she really misses him."

"Do you think she would ever accept me if you and I were to marry?"

"I'm not sure," said Heidi. "She told me once she didn't want me to ever marry again. That was shortly after Herschel died. I don't know what'd she says now. We haven't really talked about it."

"How about you? How do you feel about marriage? Do you think you could do it again?"

"I don't know, Raimund. I just don't know," exclaimed Heidi. "I'm just not ready."

"Well, I know I am – I have loved you all my life – ever since first grade."

"I love you, too, but I need some time. Memories of Herschel still torment my mind. I need more time to sort them out. I'm still tryin' to figure out why he abandoned Monika and me. Perhaps I'll never know – ya' know, that's what the scholars say – they say that no one ever really knows why they do it."

"I can wait – all I know is the last couple of years with you have been the best ones of my life. I want to be with you – I don't want anything to stop me. I'd do anything to have you and Monika accept me."

"Give us time," said Heidi. "Give us time." She reached across the table for the back of his hand and pulled it toward her lips – she kissed it softly.

# 51

December 1964

12/12. Today, we are celebrating our eighteenth anniversary for the publication of The Kourier. We celebrated with the staff this afternoon with hors d'oeuvres and wine.

12/13. My editorial on the Klein water issue has been nominated by the Colorado Press Association for its annual "Best Editorial" Award. They have their annual meeting in Denver in March. I have been attending for the last fifteen years.

12/14. Have increased our rural readership for The Kourier. Have had to hire an added worker to deliver the paper – we now have two rural delivery personnel.

12/15. I have become very attached to Heidi. I discussed marriage with her. She says she is not ready to marry again. She is still having difficulties with getting over her loss of Herschel. Is not sure that her daughter Monika would condone her marriage to another. She needed more time before considering. I've waited all my life to finally have her – as long as I am with her, I can wait.

12/16. I "ran into" Albert Klein at Emma's Diner. We exchanged hellos – nothing else. I wonder what he thinks about Heidi and me. I wonder if his views of me have affected Heidi's caution about marriage. She has never mentioned him.

12/17. My Mom has adjusted well to living with me. She gets along with Olga nicely. They watch the afternoon soap operas on TV together. She meets with her church friends regularly and is still active in the Altar and Rosary Society. Olga takes her to the 7 a.m. Mass on Tuesdays and Thursdays. She and I attend the 10 a.m. Mass on Sundays.

12/18. I thought about presenting an engagement ring to Heidi – have decided against it – don't want her to think I'm pressuring her to decide on marriage.

12/19. I asked Heidi to select a dress at Schuster's for Mom for me to give to her as a Christmas present. Heidi selected a diamond-studded pin to go with it. Unbeknownst to her, I selected a similar one for Heidi.

12/20. I will be entertaining the Knobloch family with a Christmas supper and dinner at my house. Having Emma prepare a pot of beans and rolls for Christmas Eve supper, and ham, mashed potatoes, green beans, and Waldorf salad for Christmas Day dinner. She will also bake banana cream pies for us. Will have Emma's sweet rolls for breakfast. Lukas, Kristoff, and Kurt will not make it home. Stefan, Konrad, Kerstin, Katrin, Steffi and Hanna will be here.

12/21. Have bought Mary McCarthy's best-selling novel, The Group, as a Christmas present for Heidi. It is about the lives of a group of educated women – I think she will like it. I have selected a necklace from Schuster's for her also – it has a heart-shaped pendant with several embedded diamonds.

12/22. Several siblings will arrive in Klein tomorrow. I have arranged for them to stay in the Holiday Inn on the highway outside of town.

12/23. Have finished my traditional editorial message for publication in The Kourier on Christmas Day. It is a message of hope and thankfulness.

# 52

# 𝕶𝖑𝖊𝖎𝖓 𝕶𝖔𝖚𝖗𝖎𝖊𝖗
March 22, 1965

## Editorial

Yesterday, we buried two Klein servicemen, casualties of the Vietnam War: Sgt. Fredrik Krause, US Army, and Pfc. Luther Ziegler, US Army. Both were graduates of Klein High School. Ziegler was engaged to marry, and Krause left behind a wife and two children. They are the 17$^{th}$ and 18$^{th}$ Vietnam combat victims from Klein, supplying a ratio of 1 combat death per 290 citizens compared to 1 in 600 for the rest of the nation. We in Klein, like many other small towns across America, have sent more than our share of young men to die in that foreign country. And today, it is mostly our young who are protesting the war. I received a letter from a Klein resident who is now attending Colorado University. The young man was very concerned about his country and his presumptive draft to serve in a war that he believed to be a futile cause. I have concluded it is time for me as a 39-year-old adult to be concerned about his concern and **urge the US administration to rethink its attitude toward the war and withdraw at once**. The US has gone into Vietnam for honorable and sensible purposes, but the war has turned out to be harder, longer, and more complicated than expected. I have concluded that the war is not worth winning, as South Vietnam is not absolutely imperative to American interests in Asia, and it is no longer permissible to ask young Americans to die.

# 53

At quitting time, Raimund stopped by Günther's office to chat before leaving The Kourier building. He was on his way to exercise and had changed into a hooded sweatshirt and sweatpants and sneakers.

"Boy, your Vietnam editorial sure has gotten the attention of a lot of folks," said Günther. "We've gotten over a hundred letters."

"We sure have. I'm going through them now and selecting the ones we want to publish. Many of them are from the VFW crowd. They are supporting the war."

"Yal, they are staunch patriots," said Raimund. "They think our government can do no wrong."

"Some of them are full of hate and are life threatening," said Günther. "Hard to believe that there are people out there who want to kill someone they vehemently disagree with. I almost think we're going to have to hire a bodyguard for you."

"Let's hope they aren't foolish enough to follow through on a threat they wrote in a letter," said Raimund.

"How'd you get that running outfit?" asked Günther seeing the block lettered KLEIN HIGH SCHOOL across his sweatshirt.

"Got it from the school – I substituted to teach PE for a week, and they gave me these sweats."

"I've noted that you exercise every day at this time – where do you go?"

"Bubbling Pond – it's a little over a mile around it – I run two or three laps – depending on how I feel."

"Well, have a good run."

"I will – I'll talk to you tomorrow about those letters – I want your input as to which ones we want to print."

Raimund parked his car next to the concession stand and walked to the trail on the edge of The Pond. "The temperature is just right for a nice comfortable run," said Raimund to himself as he stepped onto the sand-laden path. With short strides, he passed by the sandy beach on the eastern shore, running about a quarter of a mile where he took an abrupt turn westward to cross over the dike. On the west side, he skirted Russian olives, and bushes of lilac and currant, approaching a large cottonwood. Suddenly, from behind its trunk, a masked individual, dressed in army fatigues, a pistol in hand, jumped out in front of him, yelling,

"You f_____ing traitor!!"

He fired three shots into Raimund's mid-section. Raimund fell sideways, landing off the path into a cluster of kochia weeds. The assailant turned and ran.

Several minutes later, a frantic jogger knocked on the door of a homeowner on the north side of The Pond and yelled to him through the opened door:

"Call an ambulance! Call an ambulance! There's a man lying on the ground out here, and he's bleeding badly from the stomach! He needs a doctor – got to get him to a hospital!"

When Raimund regained consciousness, he found himself in a bed in the Logan County Hospital in Sterling. Tubes protruded from his midsection and others carried fluids into the veins of his arms. A monitor at the side of his bed recorded his heartbeat and blood pressure. Seventeen hours had passed since the bullets had entered his body. That was all he remembered – nothing else. The image of a ranting, angry soldier remained etched in his mind. He fell asleep.

When he awakened, he saw Heidi sitting beside his bed. "Hello Raimund," he heard her say.

"How long have I been here?" he asked.

"Almost 24 hours," she responded.

She grabbed his right hand and held it tightly between her palms. "You've been sleeping a lot. The doctors say you are doing very well. They say you were in good physical shape with your running and exercising."

"It is so good to see you," said Raimund. "You are always on my mind."

"For a while there, I was so afraid we were going to lose you," said Heidi. "The thought of you no longer being in my life was unbearable. I stopped in to pray for you in St. Boniface. I'd never been to that church before. Thank God my prayers have been answered."

She arose and bent over to kiss his forehead and then his lips. She placed his hand in hers and said:

"I had a conversation with Monika last night. I told her I loved you very much and wished to marry you. I told her this failed attempt to end your life has enkindled this desire even more. I told her that all the concerns I had had before about her father had been resolved in my mind, and I was now ready to marry another.

"What did she say?"

"Well, I asked her how she felt? She said, 'After all these years, I now have a better understanding and appreciation of the passion that one person can have for another, and I should not let the love I have for my father prevent my mother, the one I love dearly, from expressing her love for another'."

"She went on to say, 'I no longer disapprove of your marriage, and if I did, it would not be fair to you. Furthermore, I am certain that my father would encourage you to marry again'."

Heidi sat back down – her thoughts turned again to Raimund's serious wounds. She said to him, "They identified your attacker – was in The Kourier this morning – he turned himself in – he's an army veteran who had deployed twice to Vietnam. He's now in the Klein jail."

"Looks like Gunther is 'on top' of everything. That is good to see – it's going to be awhile before I get back in the office."

# 54

"How's your mother?" Heidi asked. "Is she still bed-ridden?"

"Yes, still hasn't overcome her paralysis – can't walk," said Raimund. She's talking much better now. That drooping paralysis on her face is starting to disappear. She likes her nurse that we've hired, so that's a good sign. She comes in every day to see her. Olga is with her all the time. Dr. Shäfer comes in once a week to check on her."

"I want to go see her. I'll try to go by next week."

"Call before you go. She likes to take naps and may be asleep."

"Is that the same side she had on her first stroke?" Heidi asked.

"Yes, it is. Dr. Shäfer is quite concerned about it."

"I hope she'll be well enough to attend the wedding," said Heidi.

"Me too. I checked with the secretary at St. Boniface to see what dates were available. She said we should nail it down soon because the June schedule is starting to fill up. Are you still sure you want to have it there?"

"I do – I want to have a small wedding. I don't want the ceremony in Zion Lutheran – it's so big. Besides, I've already done it once there. I don't want to do it again."

"Have you talked to your father about it?"

"I have not. I've only told him I'm going to marry you. He exploded. Told me he was totally against it. I'm not sure he'll even come."

"I was afraid that would be his response. I was hoping he had mellowed a bit."

"Not a chance," said Heidi. "And it's going to get worse."

"What do you mean?"

"You'll see. Just wait. My father can be a vindictive s.o.b. if he wants to."

Heidi paused to take a bite of ice cream and then resumed the conversation, "I've been looking at rings at Schuster's. I've picked out a couple for you to look at. Come by sometime, and I'll show them to you. We can decide which ones we like."

"Did you talk to your father-in-law about building a house for us?" asked Raimund.

"I did. He said he had some house plans that Herschel had done that haven't been used. He invited us to come by his office and take a look at them."

"And I talked to Tom Baker the other day. He said he has a lot on Bubbling Pond that he'd sell to us," said Raimund. "Would you like that?"

"I would as long as it isn't near my father."

"He'd be clear down the road – about a half mile. We'd be far away from him. We need to get the 'ball rolling' on this if we want to have it built before the wedding takes place."

# 55

# 𝔎𝔩𝔢𝔦𝔫 𝔎𝔬𝔲𝔯𝔦𝔢𝔯
May 7, 1965

Guest Journalist, Raimund Knobloch

## A Prairie Woman

She was born in 1901 into a family of German-via Canada immigrants on a homestead south of Fleming near the tiny settlement of St. Petersburg. She was the seventh in a family of six sisters and one son. Her father died when she was seven years old. Before his death, he had taught his daughter how to play an old organ; he whistled old hymns, and she pumped and played.

On the plains homestead, she would learn to ride horses, herd and milk cows, hoe and weed, carry water, tend chickens, to cook and bake, dress chickens, butcher cattle, to sew and darn, to grow a garden, can fruits and vegetables, to knit and crochet, and to manage a household.

Prairie life would teach her the truth and the value of faith in God. Grasshoppers, drought, hail, tornadoes, piddling prices for wheat, far horizons, family life, star-filled skies and glorious sunsets will do that to a person.

She would attend a one-room school for a total of eight years. She was attending a church picnic when she met her future husband, a Canadian-born man and a World War I veteran.

Married in 1920, the couple set out on a farm life that would take them from Fleming to Klein. Her husband would eke out a bare-bones income, just a few cents an hour, during the Great Depression. She would make do.

She would, from 1921 to 1936, bear twelve children, seven boys and five girls – including two sets of twins. Two died in early infancy; ten reached adulthood.

She was generally optimistic, fair, a good manager, slow to anger and abounding in largely unexpressed love, reticent, resourceful, a tireless worker. She would teach her children to work, to contribute to the family, not to sass, to respect their elders, to tell the truth, to be responsible, to make something of themselves.

After years of ramshackle rentals, she and her husband would scrimp and save to pay off a mortgage on a back-taxes house in Klein. She would not get her first indoor bathroom and her first electric stove until 1951. She would wait a few more years for her first electric clothes-washer – a second-hand model.

She would cook and bake and clean and sew and wash and work and teach her children from dawn to night. Twice a week, she would bake eight loaves of bread. One day, she ironed 39 shirts and blouses. She sewed beautifully. She sewed several colorful vestments for Father Gerhardt Danziger at St. Boniface Catholic Church. She made an endless number of flower-sack shirts and sheets, darned hundreds of socks and pairs of jeans, altered countless coats and pants as clothing was passed from one child to the next.

Every year, she and her children would can hundreds of quarts and pints of vegetables and fruit; all the canning was done on a coal stove in the heat of summer.

Her flower garden was beautiful, especially the cosmos.

She taught herself to play the piano and laughed with her children as she learned. She would, in the 1940s, become the organist at St. Boniface, and encouraged parishioners to sing in the choir to accompany her.

She cared for – and made her children care for – the widows and the elderly of Klein. After school evenings and Saturdays were filled with extra chores – pulling weeds, mowing lawns, shoveling snow, carrying coal, splitting wood, cleaning, and going to the Red and White store.

She would in the 1950s feel some respect from the community and begin to see her children succeed. Two served in World War II. There were high school music and academic laurels, college graduates, a career Marine, a newspaper man, scientists, a nurse, a lawyer, businessmen and businesswomen.

For cash-flow, she went to work in the school cafeteria.

She overcame paralysis from a stroke in 1950 and lost her husband in 1959 – they had been together for 39 years.

She spent her later years reading, sewing, watching television, and writing letters to children and grandchildren.

She suffered a second stroke last November, and her ten children sat with a mother who no longer knew their names.

She died two days ago, May 5, 1965, with one son and two daughters holding her hands. It was Mother's Day. I was there – you see that woman was my mother: Lara Dieffenbach Knobloch – 1901 – 1965.

I have truly been blessed. All my life, I have worked and strived to accomplish things that would please her. I only hope my efforts were not in vain.

# 56

Organist, Leona Reichert, began the prelude, and soon Raimund began to sing Ave Maria. He had sung this hymn many times at St. Boniface, but accompanied by another organist, his mother, Lara Dieffenbach Knobloch. Today, Raimund would sing the Ave Maria in honor and memory of his mother who passed away four days prior. Today he would sing with tears in his eyes and sometimes with a broken voice as he vocalized the lyrics he knew so well. In a way, Lara Knobloch was, to Raimund, very much like the Blessed Mother of Jesus – Lara accepted her life as handed down by the Lord, and Lara was virtuous. All his life, Raimund's objective had been to please Lara – to make her proud of his accomplishments. She had always been there to share in joy his achievements had brought to him. Although Lara was not known to shower another with praise, he was hopeful she applauded his work as a newspaperman. He would always remember her encouragement for him to be a writer, especially her hope that he would author a book someday that everyone in the universe would read.

All the Knobloch siblings were in attendance for Lara's final tribute. Lukas, now a lieutenant colonel, took leave from his duties in Korea and was accompanied by his Korean wife; Kristoff had started his own import business, and was working out of Hong Kong; Kurt came from Alaska where he was working with Exxon Oil as a geologist; his twin Konrad, a financial executive with MGM, arrived from LA with his wife; Stefan, teaching in a private school, drove in from Seattle; Hanna, now married to an ophthalmologist, drove in with her husband from Sterling; Kerstin, now in graduate school at UCLA, came with her boyfriend; Katrin, just out of law school, drove in from Boulder; AT&T Personnel Officer Steffi, took the train from Denver.

Fr. Gerhardt Danziger, presided over the Mass, and eulogized Lara:

"I have known Lara for most of her adult life, and in my mind, there are four characteristics that distinguish her. They are: (1) the beauty of her chosen goal in life, (2) her relentless commitment to this goal, (3) her extraordinary management skills, and (4) her religious heritage and her faith."

Fr. Gerhardt referenced the **Scriptural Proverbs 31**. "They describe Lara to a "T," he said. And then he proceeded to read them aloud:

*She brings him profit, not loss, all the days of her life.*

*She seeks out wool and flax and weaves with skilled hands.*

*She picks out a field and acquires it; from her earnings she plants a vineyard.*

*She girds herself with strength; she exerts her arms with vigor.*

*She enjoys the profit from her dealings; her lamp is never extinguished at night.*

*She puts her hands to the distaff, and her fingers ply the spindle.*

*She reaches out her hands to the poor and extends her arms to the needy.*

*She is not concerned for her household when it snows – all her charges are doubly clothed.*

*She makes her own coverlets; fine linen and purple are her clothing.*

*She is clothed with strength and dignity and laughs at the days to come.*

*She opens her mouth in wisdom; kindly instruction is on her tongue.*

*Her children rise up and call her blessed; her husband, too, praises her.*

*Many are the women of proven worth, but you have excelled them all.*

*Charm is deceptive and beauty fleeting; the woman who fears the Lord is to be praised."*

"And lastly," said Fr. Gerhardt,

*Acclaim her for the work of her hands, and let her deeds praise her at the city gates.*

"Lara deserves acclaim from the Lord for her work; he will greet her warmly at the gates of heaven," said Fr. Gerhardt.

Then Heidi and her stringed quartet played the Second Movement of Johann Sebastian Bach's Orchestral Suite No. 3 in D Major. The harmony of Bach's stringed notes produced a mournful cadence that brought tears to Heidi's eyes and loosened her mascara.

Lara was laid to rest next to Walter in the Klein Memorial Cemetery. Raimund had already supplied the headstone which read: Walter Axel Knobloch, 1895 – 1959 and Lara Dieffenbach Knobloch, 1901 –. (He would later have her year of decease carved into the stone.)

It was about noon when the final farewell prayer was said, and well-wishers and the Knoblochs reconvened at the St. Boniface reception hall where The Ladies Altar and Rosary Society supplied food and drink.

That evening, the Knoblochs assembled in a private room at Emma's for dinner. The mood was somber, but celebratory. Lara Dieffenbach Knobloch had an exemplary life. Her ten children raised their wine glasses high and drank in her memory. Raimund eulogized her once again.

# 57

Heidi took the overnight train to New York to select her outfit at Vittorio's for the wedding. She chose a pink two-piece ensemble with a knee-high skirt and a boxy pullover jacket with mid-arm sleeves and six large buttons down the front. Added to this was a pearl necklace, a pair of white gloves, a sequined purse, and high heels. She selected a white, laced veil for her head.

On June 5, 1965, pianist and celloist Hanna Kraus, recruited from the Klein Symphony Orchestra, played Pachelbel's Canon in D Major as Raimund and Heidi, arm in arm, continued down the aisle of St. Boniface Catholic Church. They were greeted at the front of the altar by presider, Fr. Gerhardt Danziger, maid of honor Monika Wenzel, and best man Günther Bernhardt.

There was a small number of attendees, mostly townspeople and friends and a few Knoblochs (Hanna and husband, Katrin, and Steffi). Notably absent was Albert Klein, although Heidi's mother, Darlene, was present. There were readings from the Old and New Testaments by the church deacon. Then Fr. Gerhardt provided a short homily:

"Heidi and Raimund have known each other since grade school, yet it has taken them more than 30 years to come together as husband and wife. The route that each has taken to this point has not been an easy one. Each of them has undergone pain and disappointment, and each has worked hard to earn each other's hand in marriage."

"**In Ecclesiastes Chapter 4, verse 9, we read: Two are better than one, because they have a good return for their labor.**"

"Yes, now in their mid-lives, now from the fruits of their past hard work, they have come to realize they will be more effective as a twosome. Yes, the Lord promises abundant bounty to those who work."

"**In Deuteronomy, Chapter 30, verses 9 and 10, it reads, "The Lord your God will make you abound in all the work of your hand, in the fruit of your body, in the increase of your livestock, and in the produce of your land for good. For the Lord will again rejoice over you for good as He rejoiced over your fathers.**""

"The genealogy of Heidi Klein Wentzel and Raimund Knobloch indicates they come from families whose hard work has contributed to the prosperity they both now enjoy. Furthermore, the Kleins, the Wentzels and the Knoblochs supplied the fine quality of life we now have in this great community we all live in. Despite their wealth and well-being, we encourage Heidi and Raimund to not let their affluence quench their love."

"**In Proverbs 3:9-10 we are told: Honor the Lord with your wealth and with the best part of everything you produce. Then he will fill your barns with grain, and your vats will overflow with good wine.**"

"Finally, I encourage them to follow the advice provided by **John in Chapter 15, verse 12: My command is this: Love each other as I have loved you.**"

Fr. Gerhardt invited them to state their intentions of marriage and to exchange their vows. He blessed the rings before they were placed on their fingers.

When instructed to do so, Raimund placed a gentle kiss on Heidi's lips. The attendees clapped with approval. Fr. Gerhardt invited all to say the Lord's Prayer with him. Then he dismissed the newlyweds with: "Go in peace to glorify the Lord with your life."

Accompanied by the music of the Canon, the wedding party recessed from the church and congregated in the adjacent assembly hall, ready to greet invitees and celebrate with refreshment. At reception end, Günther drove Heidi and Raimund to Sterling Airport where they boarded a chartered, twin-engine Cessna that flew them to Denver's Stapleton Airport. They boarded a United airliner to Los Angeles, and then another to Hawaii – they would spend two weeks on the islands.

# 58

"I'm glad the movers got our furniture here," said Heidi as she and Raimund sat down in soft chairs in the back porch of their new home on Bubbling Pond.

"Yes, at least we'll have a bed to sleep in tonight," said Raimund.

It was shortly after eight o'clock and they were sipping Chinese wine that Kristoff sent them from Hong Kong. Just getting back from Hawaii that afternoon, they were tired and exhausted and now thankful for the opportunity to finally relax. On the coffee table in front of them were plates of fried shrimp and calamari, carrot and celery and cheese sticks, and potato chips that had been delivered from Emma's Diner.

Looking over The Pond to the west, they could see the sun dropping to the horizon, surrounded by a brilliant sky of orange and yellow. Although there was no air movement, it was a comfortable mid-seventy degrees, previously cooled by a late-evening thunder shower. The refreshing smell of the rain lingered. The surface of Bubbling Pond was still and glass-like, and a ribbon of orange sunlight reflected from it. It was unusually quiet – all that could be heard was the soft roar trucks on the nearby highway. Their constant bellow was a reminder that the community of Klein was no longer a sleepy town on the prairie but was now a bustling city connected by commerce from all directions. Likewise, Bubbling Pond, which was once a diminutive water hole on the prairie, was now a gigantic pool fulfilling the domestic needs of the city as well as the agricultural demands of the surrounding rural community. Once just a stop-over spot for a stagecoach, Bubbling Pond was now a permanent residence site for thousands of folks, namely Raimund and Heidi.

"I just got off the phone talking to Mom," said Heidi. "She sez Father still hasn't gotten over our marriage. She sez he's threatening to remove me from his will and give it all to Monika. Sez he'll never speak to me again."

"Hopefully, over time, maybe he will change," said Raimund.

"I don't think he will," said Heidi. "But I'm not going to let his spiteful behavior, or his coveted wealth interfere with the happiness I'm now feeling with you. Tonight, I am the happiest I've been in a long time."

"I feel the same way," said Raimund as he turned to kiss her.

The joyous couple watched the sun disappear below the horizon as they looked over the water of Bubbling Pond. They raised their glasses and toasted their God. From his memory, Raimund recited **Proverbs 3:3-4**:

> Let love and faithfulness never leave you;
> bind them around your neck,
> write them on the tablet of your heart.
> Then you will win favor and a good name
> in the sight of God and man.

Raimund said to himself: "Someday, I am going to write about these times and this moment." Then he thought about Lara – she had encouraged him to be a writer. He had sought her approval all his life. She had been the one for whom he had worked, lived, and loved. He was confident that he would continue to receive her acclaim from her heavenly station. And now after patient pursuit, he had received the hand of a beloved – now there were two – Lara and Heidi. For Lara and

Heidi, he would continue to work, live and love. He knew he had been blessed.

www.ingramcontent.com/pod-product-compliance
Lightning Source LLC
LaVergne TN
LVHW021821060526
838201LV00058B/3476